6

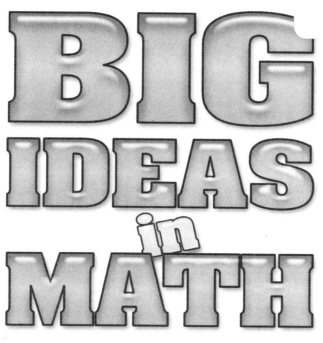

BIG IDEAS in MATH

Focal Points Support

Continental

Acknowledgments

Editorial Development: K.E. Possler
Cover Design: Joan Herring
Interior Design: Joan Herring

ISBN 978-0-8454-5594-4

TABLE of CONTENTS

INTRODUCTION

Have you ever watched a skyscraper being constructed? The building starts with the foundation, a solid base that the structure rests on. It must be very strong to hold up the rest of the building. Then the walls go up one floor at a time, each resting on the one below it. Each level must be strong enough to hold up the parts above it.

Learning math is like constructing a building. Every year you learn a great variety of things in math class. What you learn each year builds on what you learned the year before. You must master certain ideas and skills before moving on to the next level. You must understand these ideas thoroughly and be comfortable using them.

At every grade level, some ideas and skills are more important than others. These are sometimes called the "big ideas." Big ideas are valuable in themselves, but they are also crucial because they tie together many other math ideas. In grade 6, the big ideas include multiplication and division of decimals and fractions, ratios and rates, and expressions and equations.

This book, **Big Ideas in Math,** will help you build a solid math foundation. All of the lessons focus on one of the three big ideas of sixth-grade math. The lessons and practice activities guide you in understanding the big ideas in five ways.

These five ways are called process skills and refer to ways of thinking. They include:

- Representation—There are many ways to model mathematical ideas, such as objects, pictures and diagrams, words, and symbols. Models are a way to show an idea.

- Reasoning—You use reasoning when you explain why something is true. Reasoning is also involved in working out problem-solving steps.

- Connections—Mathematical ideas are linked together and build on one another. Recognizing the connections helps you use the skills in new ways.

- Communication—Mathematics has a special vocabulary. Using that language to clearly express your thinking is an important skill.

- Problem solving—A problem is something you need to find an answer for that may not be immediately obvious. To solve it, you must decide what the answer will be and how to reach it. When you apply your math skills in a step-by-step way to do this, you are solving problems.

Multiplying Decimals by 10, 100, or 1,000

Multiply decimals by 10, 100, or 1,000 the same way you multiply whole numbers by powers of 10. Place the decimal point in the product the same number of decimal places as in the decimal factor.

Read this problem. Answer each question.

Ashley read a 100-page book. Each page took her 1.8 minutes to read. How many minutes did it take Ashley to read the whole book?

$$100 \times 1.8 = 1800$$

1 Multiply: $1 \times 18 =$ _____ $10 \times 18 =$ _____ $100 \times 18 =$ _____

2 Look at the products of 18 and a power of 10. How do they change? Describe the pattern.

_____

3 Multiply 1.8 by powers of 10: $1 \times 1.8 =$ _____ $10 \times 1.8 =$ _____ $100 \times 1.8 =$ _____

4 How do the products of 1.8 and a power of 10 change? Describe the pattern.

_____

5 How many minutes did it take Ashley to read the whole book? _____ Place the decimal point in the product of the example above.

6 How many zeros are in 100? _____
How many places did the decimal point move when 1.8 was multiplied by 100? _____

7 Explain how to multiply a decimal by 10, 100, or 1,000 by using the shortcut of moving the decimal point.

_____

_____

_____

⬤ INDEPENDENT PRACTICE

Multiply.

8 $10 \times 6.35 =$ _____   **9** $100 \times 6.35 =$ _____   **10** $1,000 \times 6.35 =$ _____

11 $0.417 \times 10 =$ _____   **12** $0.417 \times 100 =$ _____   **13** $0.417 \times 1,000 =$ _____

Multiply by moving the decimal point.

14 $0.7 \times 10 =$ _____

15 $0.9 \times 100 =$ _____

16 $0.3 \times 1,000 =$ _____

17 $2.083 \times 10 =$ _____

18 $0.45 \times 100 =$ _____

19 $1.056 \times 1,000 =$ _____

20 $10 \times 36.84 =$ _____

21 $100 \times 5.05 =$ _____

22 $1,000 \times 0.789 =$ _____

Solve each problem. Show your work.

23 Pencil erasers are on sale for $0.06 each. How much would it cost Ginger to buy 100 erasers?

24 If two pencils cost $0.24, how much would 1,000 pencils cost?

25 Jorge made a stack of 10 quarters on his desk. If the thickness of each quarter is 0.069 inch, how tall is the stack?

26 There are 100 history textbooks on a table. If each one weighs 2.25 pounds, what is their total weight?

Answer each question.

27 Multiply: $0.2 \times 10 =$ _____ $0.02 \times 100 =$ _____ What decimal can be multiplied by 1,000 to get the same product as these two problems? Explain.

_____

_____

28 The total cost of 10 footballs is the same as the total cost of 100 ping-pong balls. How is the price of 1 football related to the price of 1 ping-pong ball? Explain.

_____

_____

_____

UNIT 1

7

Multiplying Decimals and Whole Numbers

Multiply decimals the same way you multiply whole numbers. Then place the decimal point to give the product the same number of decimal places as the decimal factor.

Read this problem. Answer each question.

Lamont has 5 packages to mail. Each package weighs 4.05 pounds. Lamont thinks the packages weigh a total of 202.5 pounds.

$$\begin{array}{r} 4.05 \\ \times\,5 \\ \hline 2025 \end{array}$$

1 Which two numbers should be multiplied to find the total weight? _____

2 What is the decimal factor? _____

3 How many decimal places does the decimal factor have? _____

4 What is the product without the decimal point? _____

5 How many decimal places will the product have? _____ Place the decimal point in the product in the example above.

6 What is the total weight of the packages? _____

7 What mistake did Lamont make when he found the total weight? Explain.

_____

_____

INDEPENDENT PRACTICE

Place the decimal point in each product. Answer the question.

8 $3 \times 5.8 = 174$

9 $3.9 \times 5 = 195$

10 $7 \times 20.92 = 14644$

11 $2 \times 0.25 = 050$

12 $5.61 \times 6 = 3366$

13 $9 \times 0.834 = 7506$

14 $18 \times 4.008 = 72144$

15 $0.8 \times 450 = 3600$

16 $1.54 \times 225 = 34650$

17 Add: $2.55 + 2.55 + 2.55 =$ _____ Multiply: $3 \times 2.55 =$ _____ Do the sum and the product have the same number of decimal places? Why?

_____

_____

BIG IDEAS in MATH Grade 6

Multiply.

18 6.2
   ×8

19 0.95
   ×17

20 20.7
   ×25

21 1.853
   ×3

22 0.005
   ×47

23 88
   ×0.9

24 43
   ×0.24

25 120
   ×0.4

26 500
   ×0.053

27 225
   ×1.5

Solve each problem. Show your work.

28 A case holds 24 cans of cat food. Each can weighs 6.56 ounces. How much does the case of cat food weigh, in ounces?

29 The Hope Diamond weighs about 46 carats. One carat is equal to 0.007 ounce. What is the weight of the Hope Diamond in ounces?

Solve each problem. Answer each question.

30 Multiply a decimal less than 1 and a whole number. _____

Is the product greater than or less than the whole number? Explain. _____

_____

_____

31 Multiply a decimal greater than 1 and a whole number. _____

Is the product greater than or less than the whole number? Explain. _____

_____

_____

UNIT 1

Multiplying Decimals by Decimals

Multiply decimals the same way you multiply whole numbers and decimals.

Study this model. Answer each question.

Multiply: $0.6 \times 0.4 =$

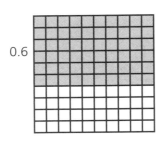
0.4
0.6

×

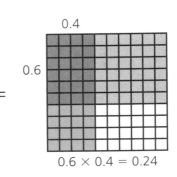
0.4
0.6

=

0.4
0.6

$0.6 \times 0.4 = 0.24$

1 How many rows are shaded in the first grid to show 0.6? _____

2 How many columns are shaded in the second grid to show 0.4? _____

3 If each row or column represents 0.1, what decimal does each square in the grid represent? _____

4 The overlap of rows and columns represents the product of 0.6×0.4. How many squares are shaded in the overlap? _____

5 What is the product of 0.6×0.4? _____

6 Explain how the total number of decimal places in the factors 0.6 and 0.4 is related to the number of decimal places in the product.

_____

_____

⬤ INDEPENDENT PRACTICE

Write a decimal multiplication sentence for each grid model.

7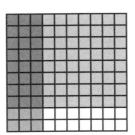

8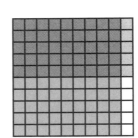

9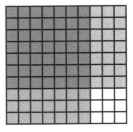

_____   _____   _____

BIG IDEAS in MATH Grade 6

Shade the grid to show each multiplication problem, and find the product.

10 $0.2 \times 0.3 =$ _____

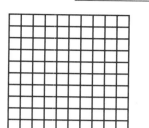

11 $0.1 \times 0.8 =$ _____

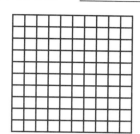

12 $0.5 \times 0.5 =$ _____

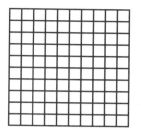

13 $0.6 \times 0.7 =$ _____

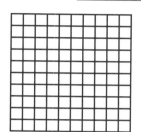

14 $0.4 \times 0.5 =$ _____

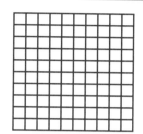

15 $0.5 \times 0.8 =$ _____

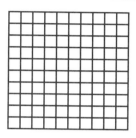

Solve each problem. Show or explain your work.

16 Lakshmi says that $0.6 \times 0.5 = 0.30$. Padma used a calculator and says that $0.6 \times 0.5 = 0.3$. Are they both correct? Explain.

_____

_____

_____

17 A city park is shaped like a rectangle 0.9 mile long and 0.7 mile wide. Use the grid to model this problem.

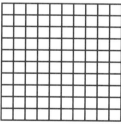

18 What is the area in square miles of the park?

_____

19 A sign in the park is 0.3 yard long and 0.6 yard wide. Use the grid to model this problem.

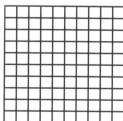

20 What is the area in square yards of the sign?

_____

More Multiplying Decimals by Decimals

Multiply two decimal factors the same way you multiply whole numbers. The number of decimal places in the product should equal the total number of decimal places in the factors.

Read this problem. Answer each question.

One mile equals approximately 1.609 kilometers. What is the length in kilometers of a racetrack that is 2.15 miles long?

$$\begin{array}{r} 1.609 \\ \times\, 2.15 \\ \hline 8045 \\ 16090 \\ 321800 \\ \hline 345935 \end{array}$$

1 How many decimal places are in 1.609? _____

2 How many decimal places are in 2.15? _____

3 What is the total number of decimal places in the factors? _____

4 What is the product without the decimal point? _____

5 How many decimal places should the product have? _____

6 How many kilometers long is the racetrack? _____

7 Is your answer reasonable? Explain how you can use estimation to find out.

_____

_____

_____

_____

● INDEPENDENT PRACTICE

Tell how many decimal places each product will have. (You don't need to find the products.)

8
$$\begin{array}{r} 3.26 \\ \times\, 0.8 \\ \hline \end{array}$$

Decimal places _____

9
$$\begin{array}{r} 74.5 \\ \times\, 37.5 \\ \hline \end{array}$$

Decimal places _____

10
$$\begin{array}{r} 0.009 \\ \times\, 0.07 \\ \hline \end{array}$$

Decimal places _____

Place the decimal point in each product.

11 $0.5 \times 1.5 = 075$

12 $21.08 \times 6.4 = 134912$

13 $3.44 \times 2.56 = 88064$

14 $0.07 \times 0.03 = 00021$

15 $5.3 \times 2.145 = 113685$

16 $0.704 \times 2.88 = 202752$

17 $1.2 \times 4.5 = 540$ or 54

18 $8.06 \times 0.5 = 403$

19 $0.05 \times 0.008 = 00004$

Multiply.

20
$$9.7 \times 2.4$$

21
$$5.82 \times 0.6$$

22
$$1.007 \times 4.3$$

23
$$4.31 \times 6.2$$

24
$$0.44 \times 0.55$$

25
$$8.036 \times 1.08$$

26
$$1.509 \times 3.4$$

27
$$0.014 \times 0.003$$

Solve each problem. Answer the question.

28 Each side of a square is 4.09 centimeters in length. What is the area, in square centimeters, of the square?

29 Peaches cost $2.35 per pound. Liza bought 2.8 pounds of peaches. What was the total cost of the peaches she bought?

30 Explain how you knew where to place the decimal point in the answer to question 29. Were there any extra zeros? Explain.

_____

_____

_____

UNIT 1

Multiplying Decimals to Solve Problems

You can multiply decimals to solve many types of word problems. Sometimes you need to change fractions or percents into decimals before multiplying.

Read this problem. Answer each question.

Watermelons are on sale for $1.44 per pound. What would be the cost of a watermelon that weighed six and three-fourths pounds?

$1.44 pound

1 What is six and three-fourths written as a decimal? _____

2 Write a multiplication expression with decimals that you could use to find the total cost of the watermelon. _____

3 Solve the problem. What is the product without the decimal point? _____

4 How many decimal places should the product have? _____

5 What is the product with the decimal point? _____

6 What will be the cost of the watermelon? _____

7 Explain how you wrote the product in dollars and cents, without any extra zeros.

_____

_____

_____

⬤ INDEPENDENT PRACTICE

Write a decimal multiplication expression you could use to solve each problem.

8 What is 35% of 80? _____

9 How far is $\frac{2}{5}$ of a 6.2-mile race? _____

10 What is the 7.5% sales tax on a $12.59 purchase? _____

11 How much is five-eighths of a $2\frac{1}{2}$-acre piece of land? _____

BIG IDEAS in MATH Grade 6

Solve each problem. Show your work. Answer each question.

12 To convert Celsius temperatures to Fahrenheit, multiply the Celsius temperature by 1.8, and then add 32. What is the Fahrenheit equivalent of a temperature of 4.6°C?

_____

13 Miguel is riding his bicycle at a speed of $\frac{1}{4}$ mile per minute. How far will he ride in 6.8 minutes?

_____

14 A $12.00 calendar is on sale for 20% off. What is the sale price of the calendar?

_____

15 A **rod** is a measure of length equal to $5\frac{1}{2}$ yards. A brick wall is $4\frac{3}{8}$ rods long. What is the length of the wall in yards?

_____

16 The flow rate of a showerhead is $2\frac{3}{4}$ gallons per minute. If this flow rate is reduced by 8%, what will be the new flow rate?

_____

17 Explain how you found the answer to question 16.

_____

_____

_____

18 Emma solved question 14 above by multiplying $12.00 by 0.8. Is Emma's strategy correct? Explain why or why not.

_____

_____

_____

Unit 1 Review

Multiply by moving the decimal point to the right.

1 $5.29 \times 10 =$ _____

2 $0.062 \times 100 =$ _____

3 $2.405 \times 1,000 =$ _____

4 $10 \times 1.8 =$ _____

5 $100 \times 3.064 =$ _____

6 $1,000 \times 0.056 =$ _____

Place the decimal point in each product. Answer the question.

7 $2.04 \times 7 = 1428$

8 $9.6 \times 5.3 = 5088$

9 $0.078 \times 4 = 0312$

10 $3.11 \times 3.06 = 95166$

11 $6.8 \times 2.05 = 1394$

12 $1.55 \times 0.004 = 00062$

13 If 3.007 is multiplied by 0.44, how many decimal places will be in the product? Explain.

_____

_____

Shade the grid to show each multiplication problem, and find the product.

14 $0.3 \times 0.5 =$ _____

15 $0.5 \times 0.9 =$ _____

16 $0.8 \times 0.8 =$ _____

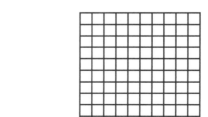

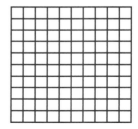

Multiply.

17
$$\begin{array}{r} 1.7 \\ \times\,0.4 \\ \hline \end{array}$$

18
$$\begin{array}{r} 5.8 \\ \times\,0.5 \\ \hline \end{array}$$

19
$$\begin{array}{r} 0.06 \\ \times\,27 \\ \hline \end{array}$$

20
$$\begin{array}{r} 3.22 \\ \times\,0.8 \\ \hline \end{array}$$

21
$$\begin{array}{r} 5.081 \\ \times\,100 \\ \hline \end{array}$$

22
$$\begin{array}{r} 8.06 \\ \times\,2.5 \\ \hline \end{array}$$

23
$$\begin{array}{r} 0.243 \\ \times\,0.65 \\ \hline \end{array}$$

24
$$\begin{array}{r} 9.44 \\ \times\,3.03 \\ \hline \end{array}$$

BIG IDEAS in MATH Grade 6

Solve each problem. Show your work. Answer each question.

25 A candle is 10 inches long. If 1 inch = 2.54 centimeters, what is the candle's length in centimeters?

_____

26 A bag of cat food weighs 3.5 pounds. What is the total weight of 6 bags of cat food?

_____

27 The top speed of an electric golf cart is 7.2 meters per second. How far could it travel in 4.9 seconds?

_____

28 Is your answer to question 27 reasonable? Show how to check it using estimation.

_____

29 A rectangular postcard measures $4\frac{1}{4}$ inches by $5\frac{1}{2}$ inches. What is the area in square inches of this postcard?

_____

30 What is 85% of 220?

_____

31 Grace bought a T-shirt priced at $8.50. If 6% sales tax was added to the price, what was the total cost?

_____

32 Find these products: 0.1 × 4.8 = _____   0.1 × 37.4 = _____
Explain how to multiply a decimal by 0.1 by moving the decimal point.

_____

_____

_____

Dividing Decimals by 10, 100, or 1,000

Divide decimals by 10, 100, or 1,000 the same way you divide whole numbers by powers of 10.

Read this problem. Answer each question.

A frog measured 7.5 centimeters in length. To find its length in meters, Davis divided by 100, the number of centimeters in 1 meter. What is the equivalent length in meters?

$$7.5 \div 100 = 0075$$

1 Divide: 75 ÷ 1 = _____   75 ÷ 100 = _____   75 ÷ 1,000 = _____

2 Look at the quotients of 75 and a power of 10. How do they change? Describe the pattern.

_____

3 Divide: 7.5 ÷ 1 = _____   7.5 ÷ 10 = _____   7.5 ÷ 1,000 = _____

4 How do the quotients of 7.5 and a power of 10 change? Describe the pattern.

_____

5 What is the frog's length in meters? _____   Place the decimal point in the example.

6 How is the quotient different from the dividend? _____

_____

7 Explain how to divide a decimal by 10, 100, or 1,000 by moving the decimal point in the dividend.

_____

_____

_____

⬤ INDEPENDENT PRACTICE

Divide.

8 4.6 ÷ 10 = _____

9 4.6 ÷ 100 = _____

10 4.6 ÷ 1,000 = _____

11 38.5 ÷ 10 = _____

12 38.5 ÷ 100 = _____

13 38.5 ÷ 1,000 = _____

14 0.2 ÷ 10 = _____

15 0.2 ÷ 100 = _____

16 0.2 ÷ 1,000 = _____

BIG IDEAS in MATH   Grade 6

Divide.

17 0.91 ÷ 10 = _____   **18** 0.6 ÷ 100 = _____   **19** 0.34 ÷ 1,000 = _____

20 44.3 ÷ 10 = _____   **21** 8.5 ÷ 100 = _____   **22** 69.7 ÷ 1,000 = _____

23 2.05 ÷ 10 = _____   **24** 12.7 ÷ 100 = _____   **25** 375.1 ÷ 1,000 = _____

Solve each problem. Show your work.

26 A slice of cheese is 8.4 millimeters thick. What is its thickness in centimeters? (1 centimeter = 10 millimeters)

27 Ms. Rainey bought 70.6 grams of cheese at a deli. How many kilograms is this? (1 kilogram = 1,000 grams)

Answer each question.

28 Multiply: 0.1 × 2.6 = _____   Divide: 2.6 ÷ 10 = _____
Does multiplying a decimal by 0.1 always give the same answer as dividing by 10? Explain.

_____

_____

_____

29 Dividing by 100 gives the same answer as multiplying by what number? Explain, and give an example.

_____

_____

_____

30 Dividing by 1,000 gives the same answer as multiplying by what number? Explain, and give an example.

_____

_____

_____

UNIT 2   **19**

Dividing Decimals by Whole Numbers

Divide decimals by whole numbers the same way you divide whole numbers. Place the decimal point in the quotient directly above the decimal point in the dividend.

Read this problem. Answer each question.

A fence measures 0.4 kilometer in length. It is divided into 8 equal sections. How long is each section of the fence?

$$
\begin{array}{r}
0 \\
8\overline{)0.4} \\
\underline{0} \\
40 \\
\underline{40} \\
0
\end{array}
$$

1 Which number is the divisor? _____

2 Which number is the dividend? _____   What place is the 4 in? _____

3 Write the decimal point in the quotient of the example. Where does the decimal point go?

_____

4 Divide $0.4 \div 8$. Think: How many times does 8 go into 4? _____
Write this number in the tenths place of the quotient in the example.

5 Write a 0 after the 4 in the dividend to make 40 hundredths.
Divide $0.40 \div 8$. Think: How many times does 8 go into 40? _____
Write this number in the hundredths place of the quotient.

6 How long is each section of the fence? _____

7 Explain how you knew when the division was complete.

_____

_____

_____

● INDEPENDENT PRACTICE

Place the decimal point in each quotient.

8 $0.36 \div 9 = 004$ **9** $2.48 \div 4 = 062$ **10** $12.084 \div 6 = 2014$

11 $0.048 \div 6 = 0008$ **12** $1.08 \div 12 = 009$ **13** $80.06 \div 20 = 4003$

14 What does a 0 to the left of the decimal point in the quotient mean? _____

_____

Divide.

15 $3\overline{)6.18}$ **16** $8\overline{)2.48}$ **17** $7\overline{)4.2}$ **18** $2\overline{)3.47}$

19 $9\overline{)3.33}$ **20** $6\overline{)3.054}$ **21** $15\overline{)0.3}$ **22** $40\overline{)48.8}$

23 $25\overline{)4.5}$ **24** $6\overline{)48.138}$ **25** $4\overline{)27.212}$ **26** $32\overline{)129.92}$

Solve each problem. Show your work.

27 Four friends bought a gift that cost $13.44. If they shared the cost equally, how much money did each friend pay?

28 The total weight of the 12 eggs in a carton is 29.4 ounces. If each egg weighs the same, what is the weight of each egg?

Answer each question.

29 Do these two division problems: $3\overline{)7.5}$ $3\overline{)0.75}$

30 How are the dividends in these problems related? How are the quotients related? Explain.

_____

_____

UNIT 2

Dividing Decimals by Decimals

A model can help you **divide a decimal by a decimal.** In the model below, each square stands for one whole that is divided into tenths.

Read this problem. Answer each question.

Divide: 2.4 ÷ 0.6 =

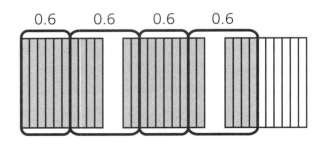

1 What decimal number does the total shaded area represent? _____

2 How many shaded tenths are inside each circled group? _____

3 What decimal number does each circled group of tenths represent? _____

4 Explain how the model shows the division problem 2.4 ÷ 0.6.

_____

_____

5 What is the quotient of 2.4 ÷ 0.6? How did you use the model to find the quotient? Explain.

_____

_____

_____

● INDEPENDENT PRACTICE

Write a decimal division sentence to match each model.

6
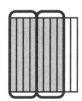

7
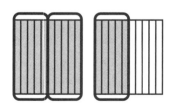

8
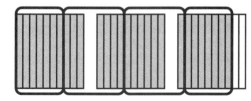

_____   _____   _____

BIG IDEAS in MATH   Grade 6

Shade the model and draw circles to show each division problem. Then find each quotient.

9 1.0 ÷ 0.5 = _____

10 1.6 ÷ 0.4 = _____

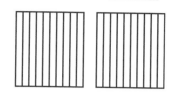

11 2.4 ÷ 0.8 = _____

12 0.9 ÷ 0.3 = _____

13 1.5 ÷ 0.3 = _____

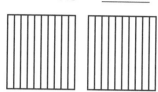

14 2.8 ÷ 0.4 = _____

Solve each problem.

15 Robert made 2.5 pounds of chocolate fudge to give as holiday gifts. He will put 0.5 pound of fudge in each gift box. How many boxes can Robert fill?

Use the model to find the quotient.

Write and solve a division sentence that represents this problem.

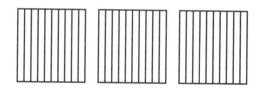

Division sentence: _____

16 Look at the division model below.

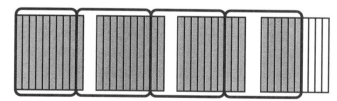

What are the two different division problems that this model represents? Explain.

Problem 1: _____   Problem 2: _____

_____

_____

_____

UNIT 2   **23**

More Dividing Decimals by Decimals

To **divide a decimal by another decimal,** first rewrite the problem so that the divisor is a whole number.

Read this problem. Answer each question.

Original problem	Step 1	Step 2	Step 3
$4.08\overline{)0.9384}$	$408.\overline{)0.9384}$	$408.\overline{)093.84}$	$408.\overline{)93.84}$

Step 3:
$$\begin{array}{r} 0 \\ 408.\overline{)93.84} \\ 816 \\ \hline 1224 \\ 1224 \end{array}$$

1 Look at the original problem. Which number is the divisor? _____

2 Look at step 1. How many places to the right must the decimal point be moved to make the divisor a whole number? _____

3 Look at step 2. How many places to the right has the decimal point in the dividend been moved? _____

4 Moving the decimal points in the divisor and dividend is the same as multiplying by what number? Explain.

_____

_____

5 Complete this sentence: 0.9384 ÷ 4.08 is equivalent to _____ ÷ _____.

6 Look at step 3. When a decimal is divided by a whole number, where should the decimal point be placed in the quotient? _____

7 Place the decimal point and complete the division in step 3. What is the quotient? _____

 INDEPENDENT PRACTICE

Divide.

8 $0.3\overline{)0.12}$ **9** $0.9\overline{)0.45}$ **10** $0.8\overline{)7.2}$ **11** $0.5\overline{)2.5}$

BIG IDEAS in MATH Grade 6

Divide.

12 $0.2\overline{)4.6}$

13 $0.6\overline{)0.54}$

14 $1.6\overline{)0.064}$

15 $0.5\overline{)3.45}$

16 $0.03\overline{)1.35}$

17 $0.12\overline{)1.08}$

18 $0.23\overline{)0.138}$

19 $0.52\overline{)1.872}$

20 $0.004\overline{)0.484}$

21 $0.007\overline{)0.266}$

22 $0.025\overline{)0.0825}$

23 $0.046\overline{)0.7774}$

Divide. Annex zeros to the dividend where you need to.

24 $0.8\overline{)0.4}$

25 $0.4\overline{)8.2}$

26 $0.02\overline{)1.7}$

27 $0.25\overline{)2.7}$

Answer this question.

28 Adrian knows that the quotient of 0.75 ÷ 0.8 is less than 1. He knows that the quotient of 0.8 ÷ 0.75 is greater than 1. Explain how Adrian can know this without doing the division.

_____

_____

_____

_____

UNIT 2

Dividing Decimals to Solve Problems

You can divide decimals to solve many types of word problems. Division situations can include measurement conversions, rate calculations, and changing a fraction to a decimal.

Read this problem. Answer each question.

A dairy cow gave 3.77 gallons of milk in one day. If 1 liter = 0.26 gallon, how many liters of milk did the cow give?

$$0.26)\overline{3.77} \quad \rightarrow \quad 26.)\overline{377.}$$

```
        26.)377.
             26
            ---
            117
            104
            ---
            130
            130
            ---
              0
```

1 How should the decimal point be moved to make the divisor a whole number?

_____

2 After the decimal points in the divisor and dividend are moved, what is the equivalent division problem? _____

3 Complete the problem at the top right. How many times does 26 go into 37? _____

4 How many times does 26 go into 117? _____

5 Why must a 0 be written after the 13? _____

6 How many liters of milk did the cow give? _____

7 Explain how you knew that the problem required division instead of multiplication.

_____

_____

_____

● INDEPENDENT PRACTICE

For each problem below, write whether it requires multiplication or division.

8 What is the decimal equivalent of $\frac{15}{24}$? _____

9 If 1 meter = 3.28 feet, then 6.5 meters is equal to how many feet? _____

10 If 10.5 pounds of cherries cost $25.20, what is the price per pound? _____

11 How many 0.25-acre lots can be made from 1.9 acres of land? _____

Solve each problem. Show your work. Answer each question.

12 A load of pressed olives yielded 85.5 liters of oil. The oil was bottled in 1.5-liter cans. How many cans were filled?

_____

13 An atom in a physics experiment traveled exactly 5.577 inches. If 1 centimeter = 0.39 inch, how many centimeters did the atom travel?

_____

14 Another atom in a physics experiment traveled 6.24 inches in 0.008 second. What was its rate of speed in feet per second?

_____

15 Explain how you found the answer to question 14.

_____

_____

_____

16 Kevin bought $2\frac{1}{20}$ pounds of tomatoes. The total cost was $5.74. What was the cost per pound of the tomatoes?

_____

17 Look at question 16. Suppose Kevin's friend Lacy bought some tomatoes that cost a total of $8.82. Explain how you could find how many pounds of tomatoes Lacy bought.

_____

_____

_____

Unit 2 Review

Divide by moving the decimal point to the left.

1 43.8 ÷ 10 = _____ **2** 43.8 ÷ 100 = _____ **3** 43.8 ÷ 1,000 = _____

4 0.1 ÷ 10 = _____ **5** 0.1 ÷ 100 = _____ **6** 0.1 ÷ 1,000 = _____

Place the decimal point in each quotient.

7 0.56 ÷ 8 = 0 0 7 **8** 3.12 ÷ 6 = 0 5 2 **9** 12.18 ÷ 4 = 3 0 4 5

Divide.

10 4)‾2.36‾ **11** 8)‾0.76‾ **12** 18)‾6.12‾ **13** 35)‾2.03‾

Shade the model and draw circles to show each division problem. Then find each quotient.

14 0.6 ÷ 0.2 = _____ **15** 1.8 ÷ 0.3 = _____ **16** 2.4 ÷ 0.4 = _____

 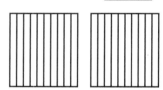 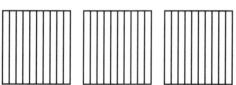

Divide.

17 0.7)‾2.1‾ **18** 0.5)‾0.35‾ **19** 2.2)‾0.088‾ **20** 0.04)‾3.84‾

21 0.06)‾0.039‾ **22** 0.008)‾0.96‾ **23** 0.015)‾0.036‾ **24** 0.24)‾0.0732‾

BIG IDEAS in MATH Grade 6

Solve each problem. Show your work. Answer each question.

25 Rosalina rode her scooter 27.6 meters in 6 seconds. What was her average speed in meters per second?

26 A large chocolate bar weighs 6.5 pounds. It will be divided equally into 100 squares. How much will each square weigh?

27 Fiona poured 0.3 liter of lemonade into each glass on the table, using 2.7 liters in all. How many glasses did she fill?

Use the model to find the quotient.

Write and solve a division sentence that represents this problem.

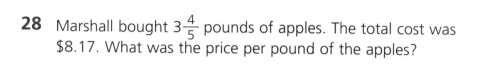

Division sentence: _____

28 Marshall bought $3\frac{4}{5}$ pounds of apples. The total cost was $8.17. What was the price per pound of the apples?

_____

29 Use estimation to check if your answer to question 28 is reasonable. Explain.

_____

_____

_____

30 Complete the three division problems:

$$0.2\overline{)1.6} \qquad 0.2\overline{)0.16} \qquad 0.2\overline{)0.016}$$

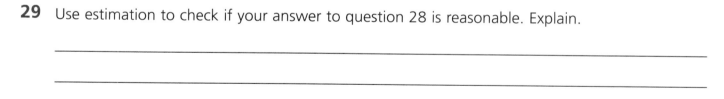

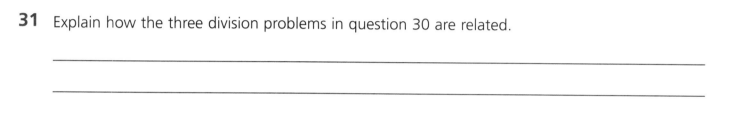

31 Explain how the three division problems in question 30 are related.

_____

_____

_____

Representing Fractions

A **fraction** can show part of a whole or part of a set. The **numerator** is the number on top. The **denominator** is the number on the bottom. A **mixed number** is a whole number plus a fraction.

Read these problems. Answer each question.

What fraction is represented by this area model?

What mixed number is marked X on this number line?

1 How many squares are in the area model? _____ This is the denominator of the fraction.

2 How many of the squares are shaded? _____ This is the numerator of the fraction.

3 What fraction is represented by the area model? _____

4 What two whole numbers is X between on the number line? _____

5 How many sections is the number line divided into between 1 and 2? _____

6 What mixed number does X represent? _____

7 Explain how you knew what mixed number X represents.

_____

_____

_____

⬤ INDEPENDENT PRACTICE

Identify the fraction or mixed number shown by each model.

8

9

10

_____   _____   _____

11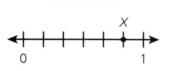

12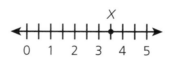

13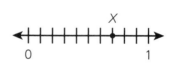

_____   _____   _____

BIG IDEAS in MATH Grade 6

Shade each area model to represent the fraction or mixed number.

14 $\frac{2}{7}$  **15** $\frac{1}{3}$ 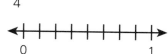 **16** $1\frac{4}{5}$

Mark each fraction or mixed number with a dot on the number line.

17 $\frac{3}{8}$

18 $\frac{3}{4}$

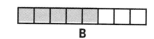

19 $1\frac{1}{2}$

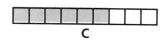

Answer each question.

20 Look at these three fraction models.

 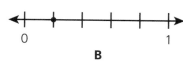 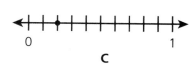

Which two of the models represent the same fraction? Explain how you know.

_____

_____

21 Look at the fractions marked on these number lines.

Which two number lines are marked with equivalent fractions? Explain how you know.

_____

_____

22 Divide and write your answer as a decimal: 4 ÷ 5 = _____

Shade $\frac{4}{5}$ of each of these area models: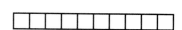

Explain how the second area model above shows the decimal answer to the division 4 ÷ 5.

_____

_____

_____

Multiplying Fractions and Whole Numbers

To **multiply a fraction by a whole number,** first write the whole number as a fraction. Then multiply the numerators and denominators. If necessary, simplify the resulting fraction.

Read this problem. Answer each question.

Marta had 4 pounds of clay. She used $\frac{3}{8}$ of the clay to make a bowl. How much clay did Marta use?

$$\frac{3}{8} \times 4 = \frac{3}{8} \times \text{\_\_\_} = \text{\_\_\_}$$

1 What is $\frac{3}{8}$ of 4 written as a multiplication expression? _____

2 What is 4 written as an improper fraction? _____   Write it in the equation above.

3 What is the product of the numerators? _____   Write it in the numerator of the product above.

4 What is the product of the denominators? _____ Write it in the denominator of the product.

5 What is the product of $\frac{3}{8}$ and 4? _____

6 What is the answer written as a mixed number in simplest terms? _____

7 A fraction is another way to write a division problem. How does that statement help explain why an improper fraction with a denominator of 1 can represent a whole number?

_____

_____

_____

● INDEPENDENT PRACTICE

Write each whole number as an improper fraction.

8 9 = _____   **9** 2 = _____   **10** 6 = _____   **11** 12 = _____

Complete.

12 $\frac{1}{2} \times 6 = \frac{1}{2} \times \text{\_\_\_} =$ **13** $\frac{2}{7} \times 3 = \frac{2}{7} \times \text{\_\_\_} =$

BIG IDEAS in MATH Grade 6

Multiply.

14 $6 \times \frac{1}{9} =$

15 $\frac{2}{3} \times 8 =$

16 $7 \times \frac{1}{2} =$

17 $2 \times \frac{5}{8} =$

18 $\frac{5}{12} \times 6 =$

19 $\frac{4}{5} \times 3 =$

20 $4 \times \frac{3}{2} =$

21 $10 \times \frac{4}{3} =$

22 $\frac{5}{4} \times 6 =$

Write each expression as a multiplication problem. Then solve.

23 $\frac{1}{8}$ of 24 hours

24 $\frac{2}{3}$ of 12 gallons

Solve each problem. Show your work. Answer each question.

25 Mr. Kung bought 5 gallons of juice for a party. Afterward, $\frac{3}{10}$ of the juice was left. How much juice was used at the party?

26 Everything at a clothing store is on sale for $\frac{1}{4}$ off. What is the sale price of a dress with a regular price of $30?

27 What is $\frac{1}{10}$ of 5? _____ How could you use this fact to answer question 25?

_____

_____

_____

28 Chelsea went to the clothing store sale described in question 26. To find the sale price of a skirt, she multiplied its regular price by $\frac{3}{4}$. Was this a correct method for finding the sale price? Explain.

_____

_____

_____

UNIT 3   **33**

Multiplying Fractions

To **multiply fractions,** multiply the numerators, multiply the denominators, and simplify if necessary. An area model can help you understand multiplying fractions.

Read this problem. Answer each question.

Multiply $\frac{5}{6} \times \frac{3}{8}$.

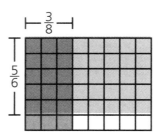

1 How many rows are in the area model? _____
   How many rows are shaded purple to represent the fraction $\frac{5}{6}$? _____

2 How many columns are in the area model? _____
   How many columns are shaded gray to represent the fraction $\frac{3}{8}$? _____

3 What is the total number of squares in the area model? _____

4 How many squares are in the intersection of the shaded rows and columns? _____

5 What fraction of the area model is shaded? _____

6 What is the product reduced to simplest form? _____

7 How are the numerators and denominators of fractions represented in an area model?

_____

_____

_____

⬤ INDEPENDENT PRACTICE

Write the fraction multiplication sentence shown by each area model. Then solve.

8   　　　 9   　　　 10

_____ 　　　 _____ 　　　 _____

Shade each area model to represent the given multiplication problem. Then solve.

11 $\frac{1}{3} \times \frac{5}{8} =$

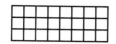

12 $\frac{3}{5} \times \frac{5}{6} =$

13 $\frac{3}{4} \times \frac{7}{8} =$

Multiply. Write each product in simplest form.

14 $\frac{1}{2} \times \frac{3}{8} =$

15 $\frac{2}{5} \times \frac{2}{3} =$

16 $\frac{3}{2} \times \frac{4}{7} =$

17 $\frac{5}{12} \times \frac{2}{3} =$

18 $\frac{3}{4} \times \frac{8}{3} =$

19 $\frac{5}{4} \times \frac{3}{2} =$

20 $\frac{1}{8} \times \frac{6}{7} =$

21 $\frac{5}{6} \times \frac{4}{9} =$

22 $\frac{8}{5} \times \frac{10}{3} =$

Solve each problem. Show your work.

23 Ando loaded $\frac{7}{12}$ ton of fertilizer onto his truck. He spread $\frac{3}{5}$ of the load on his garden. How much fertilizer did Ando use?

24 Two subway stations are $\frac{7}{4}$ miles apart. A train stopped after traveling $\frac{1}{3}$ of this distance. How far from the next station was the train when it stopped?

Answer the question.

25 Doug used a 6 × 10 grid to multiply $\frac{4}{6} \times \frac{6}{10}$. Todd used a 3 × 5 grid to do the same multiplication problem. Explain how they could use different grids to get the same answer.

_____

_____

_____

_____

A Shortcut for Multiplying Fractions

Sometimes you can **cancel common factors** before multiplying fractions. If you cancel all the common factors before multiplying, the product will be in lowest terms.

Read this problem. Answer each question.

Ruby gave $\frac{5}{6}$ pound of dog food to her dog. The dog ate $\frac{9}{10}$ of the food. How much food did Ruby's dog eat?

$$\frac{9}{10} \times \frac{5}{6} = \frac{\overset{3}{\cancel{9}}}{\underset{2}{\cancel{10}}} \times \frac{\overset{1}{\cancel{5}}}{\underset{2}{\cancel{6}}} =$$

1   Look at the numerator 9 and the denominator 6.
    What is the greatest common factor (GCF) of 9 and 6? _____

2   Look at the denominator 10 and the numerator 5. What is the GCF of 5 and 10? _____

3   Divide 9 and 6 by their GCF, and divide 5 and 10 by their GCF. This is canceling common factors. What simpler multiplication problem is the result? _____

4   Multiply the simpler problem. How much food did Ruby's dog eat? _____

5   Multiply $\frac{9}{10} \times \frac{5}{6}$ **without** first canceling common factors. What is the product? _____

6   Simplify the product from question 5. Is it the same answer as for question 4? Explain why.

_____

_____

⬤ INDEPENDENT PRACTICE

Identify the greatest common factor (GCF) of each pair of numbers.

7   4 and 8: _____   8   12 and 3: _____   9   6 and 6: _____   10   20 and 12: _____

Rewrite each multiplication problem in simpler form by canceling common factors.

11   $\frac{3}{4} \times \frac{5}{6} =$ 12 $\frac{2}{3} \times \frac{3}{8} =$ 13 $\frac{9}{8} \times \frac{4}{15} =$

BIG IDEAS in MATH   Grade 6

Multiply by canceling common factors.

14 $\frac{2}{5} \times \frac{1}{2} =$

15 $\frac{5}{8} \times \frac{2}{15} =$

16 $\frac{4}{3} \times \frac{9}{2} =$

17 $\frac{4}{7} \times \frac{3}{8} =$

18 $\frac{5}{12} \times \frac{9}{10} =$

19 $\frac{5}{6} \times \frac{4}{15} =$

20 $\frac{9}{4} \times \frac{8}{15} =$

21 $\frac{7}{10} \times \frac{10}{7} =$

22 $\frac{3}{10} \times \frac{5}{24} =$

Solve each problem. Show your work.

23 A running race was $\frac{10}{3}$ miles long. Dexter took the lead after completing $\frac{6}{25}$ of the race. How far had he run at that point?

24 It took Nikki $\frac{5}{12}$ hour to do her homework. It took Kristen $\frac{3}{5}$ as long. How long did it take Kristen to do her homework?

Answer each question.

25 There are two common factors that can be canceled before multiplying $\frac{3}{4} \times \frac{8}{9}$. If you cancel only one of the common factors, will you still get the correct product? Explain.

_____

_____

26 If two improper fractions are multiplied, can the product be less than 1? Explain.

_____

_____

27 Solve question 14 above by changing each fraction to a decimal and then multiplying. Do you get the same answer? Explain.

_____

_____

UNIT 3

Multiplying Fractions and Mixed Numbers

To **multiply a mixed number by a fraction,** you can use the distributive property.

Read this problem. Answer each question.

A trail is $3\frac{1}{4}$ kilometers long. The first $\frac{2}{5}$ of the trail is uphill. What distance is uphill?

Multiply: $\frac{2}{5} \times 3\frac{1}{4} =$

1 What is $3\frac{1}{4}$ written as a whole number plus a fraction? _____

2 The distributive property says $a \times (b + c) = (a \times b) + (a \times c)$. Explain what this means in words.

_____

_____

_____

3 Use the distributive property to rewrite $\frac{2}{5} \times 3\frac{1}{4}$: _____

4 What is the product of $\frac{2}{5} \times 3$? _____ What is the product of $\frac{2}{5} \times \frac{1}{4}$? _____

5 Write an addition expression to find the sum of the products in question 4. _____

6 What distance is uphill? Write the answer as a mixed number in simplest form. _____

7 Another way to multiply $\frac{2}{5} \times 3\frac{1}{4}$ is to change $3\frac{1}{4}$ to an improper fraction, and then multiply. Show how to find the answer using this method.

_____

 INDEPENDENT PRACTICE

Multiply using the distributive property. Write each answer in lowest terms.

8 $\frac{2}{3} \times 4\frac{1}{2} =$

9 $\frac{1}{2} \times 3\frac{1}{4} =$

10 $\frac{3}{4} \times 8\frac{2}{5} =$

11 $\frac{4}{5} \times 2\frac{5}{8} =$

12 $\frac{5}{6} \times 3\frac{2}{3} =$

13 $\frac{3}{8} \times 4\frac{1}{6} =$

BIG IDEAS in MATH Grade 6

Change each mixed number to an improper fraction.

14 $2\frac{1}{3} =$

15 $1\frac{7}{8} =$

16 $4\frac{5}{6} =$

17 $5\frac{2}{5} =$

Change each mixed number to an improper fraction and multiply. Write each answer as a fraction or mixed number in lowest terms.

18 $1\frac{1}{4} \times \frac{1}{8} =$

19 $2\frac{1}{2} \times \frac{2}{5} =$

20 $1\frac{4}{5} \times \frac{1}{3} =$

21 $\frac{5}{6} \times 2\frac{2}{5} =$

22 $\frac{7}{8} \times 2\frac{2}{3} =$

23 $\frac{3}{4} \times 3\frac{1}{5} =$

24 $1\frac{1}{2} \times 1\frac{3}{4} =$

25 $2\frac{2}{3} \times 3\frac{1}{8} =$

26 $4\frac{1}{2} \times 4\frac{2}{3} =$

Answer each question.

27 Karly is going to multiply $\frac{3}{4} \times 7\frac{5}{6}$. She wrote $7\frac{5}{6}$ as $(8 - \frac{1}{6})$ and will use the distributive property. Explain how this will work.

_____

_____

_____

28 To multiply $2\frac{1}{2} \times 3\frac{4}{5}$ using the distributive property, you would have to perform four separate multiplications, and then add the results. Explain.

_____

_____

_____

UNIT 3

Multiplying Fractions to Solve Problems

Many types of word problems can be solved by multiplying fractions or mixed numbers.

Read this problem. Answer each question.

Pedro caught a fish that was $9\frac{3}{4}$ inches long.
Tomas caught a fish $\frac{2}{3}$ as long as Pedro's.
If 1 inch equals about $2\frac{1}{2}$ centimeters, about
how many centimeters long was Tomas's fish?

$$1 \text{ inch} = 2\frac{1}{2} \text{ centimeters}$$

1 How can you find a length that is $\frac{2}{3}$ of $9\frac{3}{4}$? _____

2 What is $9\frac{3}{4}$ written as an improper fraction? _____

3 Cancel the common factors and multiply: $\frac{2}{3} \times \frac{39}{4} =$ _____

4 The rate 1 inch to $2\frac{1}{2}$ centimeters is a conversion rate.
How do you convert length from inches to centimeters? _____

5 Write an expression to multiply the product of question 3
and the conversion rate. Then multiply to find the product: _____

6 What is the length of Tomas's fish in centimeters? _____

7 Tomas solved this problem by multiplying $9\frac{3}{4}$ by $2\frac{1}{2}$, and then multiplying the product by $\frac{2}{3}$.
Is this a correct way to solve the problem? Explain.

_____

_____

_____

INDEPENDENT PRACTICE

Solve each problem. Show your work. Answer each question.

8 A pine tree is $6\frac{2}{3}$ meters tall. An oak tree is $\frac{9}{10}$ as tall as the
pine tree. How tall is the oak tree?

_____

9 At a school, $\frac{3}{8}$ of the students are studying Spanish. Of these students, $\frac{1}{6}$ are also studying Chinese. What fraction of the students at the school are studying **both** Spanish and Chinese?

_____

10 A snowboard race is $2\frac{3}{4}$ miles long. If 1 mile = $1\frac{3}{5}$ kilometers, what is the length of the race in kilometers?

_____

11 Mr. Curtis bought $\frac{5}{8}$ ton of bricks. He put the bricks in 15 equal stacks and used 4 of the stacks to build a wall. What fraction of a ton of bricks did Mr. Curtis use to build the wall?

_____

12 A box contained $\frac{3}{4}$ pound of cereal. Diamond ate one-eighth of the cereal for breakfast. How much cereal was left in the box?

_____

13 Explain how you found the answer to question 12 above.

_____

_____

_____

14 If 1 kilometer = $\frac{5}{8}$ mile, explain how you could use multiplication to check your answer to question 10 above.

_____

_____

_____

Unit 3 Review

Identify the fraction or mixed number shown by each model.

1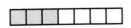

_____

2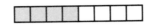

_____

3

_____

Mark each fraction or mixed number with a dot on the number line.

4 $\frac{1}{4}$

5 $2\frac{1}{3}$

6 $\frac{4}{5}$

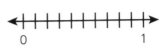

Multiply.

7 $\frac{1}{4} \times 12 =$

8 $7 \times \frac{2}{3} =$

9 $\frac{5}{6} \times 3 =$

Write the fraction multiplication sentence shown by each area model. Then solve.

10

_____

11

_____

12

_____

Multiply. Write each product in simplest form.

13 $\frac{1}{3} \times \frac{3}{5} =$

14 $\frac{3}{4} \times \frac{2}{3} =$

15 $\frac{4}{5} \times \frac{3}{7} =$

16 $\frac{5}{8} \times \frac{4}{15} =$

17 $\frac{3}{2} \times \frac{7}{3} =$

18 $\frac{5}{12} \times \frac{8}{25} =$

19 $\frac{4}{9} \times \frac{15}{8} =$

20 $\frac{7}{8} \times \frac{8}{7} =$

21 $\frac{9}{5} \times \frac{10}{3} =$

BIG IDEAS in MATH   Grade 6

Multiply using the distributive property or by changing mixed numbers to improper fractions. Write each answer as a fraction or mixed number in lowest terms.

22 $\frac{1}{3} \times 6\frac{1}{2} =$

23 $\frac{2}{5} \times 5\frac{3}{4} =$

24 $\frac{7}{12} \times 1\frac{1}{7} =$

25 $\frac{3}{10} \times 4\frac{1}{6} =$

26 $1\frac{3}{8} \times 3\frac{1}{5} =$

27 $2\frac{2}{5} \times 3\frac{3}{4} =$

Solve each problem. Show your work. Answer each question.

28 George painted $\frac{4}{9}$ of a fence. James painted $\frac{7}{8}$ as much as George. What fraction of the fence did James paint?

_____

29 A magazine article is $7\frac{1}{2}$ pages long. Neela read $\frac{5}{6}$ of the article. How many pages did she read?

_____

30 The area of a triangle equals $\frac{1}{2} \times$ base $\times$ height. If a triangle has base $4\frac{2}{5}$ feet and height $8\frac{1}{3}$ feet, what is its area?

_____

31 Tell how you found your answer to question 30 above. Could you have multiplied in a different order and still gotten the correct answer? Explain.

_____

_____

_____

UNIT 3

43

Understanding Reciprocals

When any number is multiplied by its **reciprocal,** the product is 1. To find the reciprocal of a fraction, switch the numerator and denominator.

Read this problem. Answer each question.

What is the result of multiplying $\frac{3}{5}$ by its reciprocal?

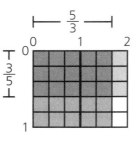

1 What is the reciprocal of $\frac{3}{5}$? _____

2 How do the rows shaded purple on the area model represent $\frac{3}{5}$? _____

_____

3 How do the columns shaded gray on the area model represent $\frac{5}{3}$? _____

_____

4 The entire model shows 2 wholes. How many squares are in 1 whole? _____

5 How many squares are shaded **both** colors to show $\frac{3}{5} \times \frac{5}{3}$? _____

6 Explain why the area model shows that $\frac{3}{5} \times \frac{5}{3} = 1$.

_____

_____

_____

● INDEPENDENT PRACTICE

Write the multiplication sentence shown by each area model.

7

8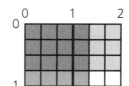

9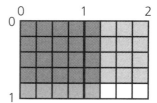

_____   _____   _____

BIG IDEAS in MATH Grade 6

Shade each area model to show the multiplication of reciprocals.

10 $\frac{2}{3} \times \frac{3}{2} = 1$

11 $\frac{5}{6} \times \frac{6}{5} = 1$

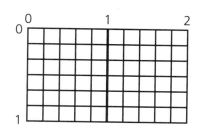

12 $\frac{2}{5} \times \frac{5}{2} = 1$

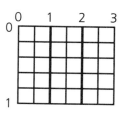

Write the reciprocal of each fraction.

13 $\frac{3}{8}$

14 $\frac{5}{9}$

15 $\frac{7}{12}$

16 $\frac{7}{3}$

17 $\frac{8}{5}$

18 $\frac{5}{3}$

19 $\frac{1}{4}$

20 $\frac{1}{9}$

Change each mixed number to an improper fraction. Then write the reciprocal.

21 $1\frac{1}{4}$

22 $3\frac{1}{2}$

23 $1\frac{7}{8}$

24 $5\frac{2}{3}$

25 $2\frac{4}{5}$

26 $3\frac{1}{6}$

27 $5\frac{3}{8}$

28 $4\frac{2}{9}$

Answer each question.

29 Choose a number and divide it by itself. _____ What is the quotient? _____

30 Multiply your number by its reciprocal. _____ What is the product? _____

31 What do your answers to questions 29 and 30 suggest about the relationship between multiplication and division?

_____

_____

_____

UNIT 4

45

Dividing Whole Numbers by Fractions

To **divide a whole number by a fraction,** multiply the whole number by the reciprocal of the fraction.

Read this problem. Answer each question.

It takes Tish $\frac{2}{3}$ of an hour to tune up a motorcycle. How many motorcycles could she tune up in 4 hours?

Divide: $4 \div \frac{2}{3} =$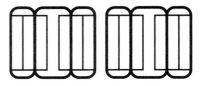

1 Which number is the dividend? _____ Which is the divisor? _____

2 The area model has 4 rectangles. What do the rectangles represent? _____
_____

3 Each circle goes around two-thirds of a rectangle. What does a circle represent? _____
_____

4 How does the area model show the quotient of $4 \div \frac{2}{3}$? _____
_____
_____

5 Dividing by a fraction is the same as multiplying by its reciprocal. What is the reciprocal of the divisor? _____

6 Rewrite $4 \div \frac{2}{3}$ as a multiplication problem and solve. _____

⬤ INDEPENDENT PRACTICE

Write the division sentence shown by each area model.

7    **8** 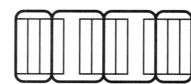   **9**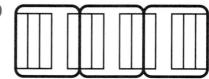

_____   _____   _____

BIG IDEAS in MATH Grade 6

Draw an area model for each division sentence.

10 $3 \div \frac{3}{2} = 2$

11 $2 \div \frac{2}{5} = 5$

12 $4 \div \frac{1}{3} = 12$

Rewrite each division as multiplication by the reciprocal. Then solve.

13 $5 \div \frac{5}{2} =$

14 $2 \div \frac{3}{4} =$

15 $6 \div \frac{3}{5} =$

16 $6 \div \frac{4}{3} =$

17 $3 \div \frac{5}{6} =$

18 $7 \div \frac{7}{8} =$

19 $5 \div \frac{1}{2} =$

20 $4 \div \frac{1}{8} =$

21 $10 \div \frac{4}{5} =$

Solve each problem. Show your work. Answer the question.

22 Gloria has 3 pounds of hamburger meat. How many $\frac{1}{4}$-pound hamburgers can she make?

23 Sasha picked 12 pounds of blackberries. How many $\frac{3}{4}$-pound baskets can she fill with these blackberries?

24 A fraction is a way of writing a division expression. For example, $\frac{3}{4}$ is the same as $3 \div 4$. Explain how $3 \div 4 = \frac{3}{4}$ is related to $3 \div \frac{3}{4} = 4$. (Hint: How is $12 \div 6 = 2$ related to $12 \div 2 = 6$?)

_____

_____

_____

UNIT 4

47

Dividing Fractions by Fractions

To **divide a fraction by another fraction,** multiply the first fraction by the reciprocal of the second fraction. An area model can help you understand division of fractions.

Read this problem. Answer each question.

Keiko and Nobu each have $\frac{3}{4}$ pound of trail mix. Keiko will put hers into bags holding $\frac{1}{6}$ pound. Nobu will put his into bags holding $\frac{5}{6}$ pound. How many bags will each person make?

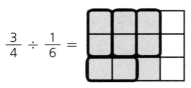

$\frac{3}{4} \div \frac{1}{6} =$

Figure 1

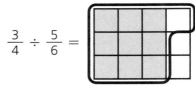

$\frac{3}{4} \div \frac{5}{6} =$

Figure 2

1 What is the least common multiple (LCM) of 4 and 6? _____

2 In a rectangle with 12 squares, how many should be shaded to show $\frac{3}{4}$? _____

3 Look at figure 1. How many of the 12 squares are circled to show $\frac{1}{6}$? _____

4 What is 9 ÷ 2? _____ Explain why this gives the answer to $\frac{3}{4} \div \frac{1}{6}$. _____

_____

5 Look at figure 2. How many of the 12 squares are circled to show $\frac{5}{6}$? _____

6 What is 9 ÷ 10? _____ Explain why this gives the answer to $\frac{3}{4} \div \frac{5}{6}$. _____

_____

7 Show how to solve these problems by multiplying by the reciprocal.

$\frac{3}{4} \div \frac{1}{6} =$ _____ $\frac{3}{4} \div \frac{5}{6} =$ _____

 INDEPENDENT PRACTICE

Write the fraction division sentence shown by each area model. Then solve.

8
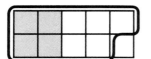

9
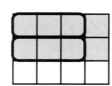

10
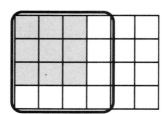

_____   _____   _____

BIG IDEAS in MATH   Grade 6

Shade each model and draw one or more circles to show each division problem. Then solve.

11 $\frac{7}{8} \div \frac{1}{2} =$

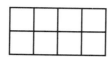

12 $\frac{5}{6} \div \frac{2}{9} =$

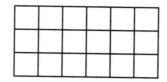

13 $\frac{1}{4} \div \frac{4}{5} =$

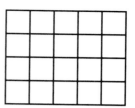

Rewrite each division as multiplication by the reciprocal. Then solve.

14 $\frac{2}{5} \div \frac{3}{4} =$

15 $\frac{3}{8} \div \frac{1}{2} =$

16 $\frac{9}{10} \div \frac{2}{7} =$

17 $\frac{2}{3} \div \frac{1}{6} =$

18 $\frac{7}{4} \div \frac{2}{3} =$

19 $\frac{7}{10} \div \frac{4}{5} =$

20 $\frac{5}{8} \div \frac{9}{2} =$

21 $\frac{4}{9} \div \frac{8}{3} =$

22 $\frac{3}{4} \div \frac{5}{12} =$

Answer each question.

23 In the division problem $\frac{3}{4} \div \frac{2}{5}$, the divisor is less than the dividend. Will the quotient be greater or less than 1? Explain how you know.

_____

_____

_____

24 In the division problem $\frac{1}{6} \div \frac{5}{8}$, the divisor is greater than the dividend. Will the quotient be greater or less than 1? Explain how you know.

_____

_____

_____

UNIT 4

Dividing Fractions by Whole Numbers

To **divide a fraction by a whole number,** multiply by the reciprocal of the whole number. To find the reciprocal of a whole number, first write the whole number as a fraction.

Read this problem. Answer each question.

Hannah cut a $\frac{6}{7}$-pound block of cheese into 4 equal pieces. What was the weight of each piece?

Divide: $\frac{6}{7} \div 4 =$

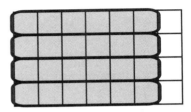

1   What division problem do you need to solve? _____

2   What is 4 written as a fraction? _____

3   What is the reciprocal of 4? _____

4   What is $\frac{6}{7} \div 4$ written as a multiplication problem? _____

5   What was the weight of each piece of cheese? _____

6   What is the LCM of 4 and 7? _____

7   How does the area model above show that $\frac{6}{7} \div 4 = \frac{3}{14}$? Explain. _____

_____

_____

_____

INDEPENDENT PRACTICE

Write the division sentence shown by each area model. Then solve.

8

9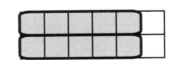

10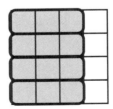

_____   _____   _____

Find the reciprocal of each whole number.

11 7　　　　　　**12** 2　　　　　　**13** 8　　　　　　**14** 20

Rewrite each division as multiplication by the reciprocal. Then solve.

15 $\frac{2}{3} \div 4 =$　　　　　　**16** $\frac{3}{8} \div \frac{3}{4} =$　　　　　　**17** $\frac{2}{5} \div 6 =$

18 $\frac{7}{15} \div \frac{1}{5} =$　　　　　　**19** $\frac{3}{4} \div 9 =$　　　　　　**20** $\frac{4}{5} \div \frac{6}{7} =$

21 $\frac{8}{3} \div 4 =$　　　　　　**22** $\frac{5}{9} \div \frac{5}{9} =$　　　　　　**23** $\frac{12}{5} \div \frac{8}{15} =$

Solve each problem. Show your work. Answer each question.

24 It took Marci $\frac{3}{4}$ hour to run 5 laps around her school. Each lap took the same amount of time. What fraction of an hour did each lap take?

25 Nine-tenths of a pizza was left in the refrigerator. Three people shared the pizza equally. What fraction of the whole pizza did each person get?

26 The picture shows a square divided into fourths. One fourth is divided into 5 equal rectangles. What fraction of the whole square is shaded? Explain how you know.

_____

_____

_____

UNIT 4

Dividing Fractions and Mixed Numbers

If a division problem involves mixed numbers, change them to improper fractions. Then multiply by the reciprocal of the divisor.

Read this problem. Answer each question.

A tract of land is $4\frac{1}{2}$ acres in size. It will be divided into lots that are $2\frac{5}{6}$ acres in size. How many lots of that size can be made?

Divide: $4\frac{1}{2} \div 2\frac{5}{6} =$

1 How many $\frac{1}{2}$s are in 4? _____ Write 4 as a fraction with a denominator of 2. _____

2 Add $\frac{1}{2}$ to the improper fraction for 4 to get $4\frac{1}{2}$ written as an improper fraction. _____

3 How you can use multiplication and addition to change a mixed number to an improper

fraction? Explain. _____

_____

4 Multiply and add to change $2\frac{5}{6}$ to an improper fraction. _____

5 Rewrite the division problem as multiplication by the reciprocal. _____

6 Cancel common factors and multiply. Write the product as a mixed number.

_____

7 What would be the result of multiplying $1\frac{10}{17}$ by $2\frac{5}{6}$? Explain how you know. _____

_____

⬤ INDEPENDENT PRACTICE

Change each mixed number to an improper fraction.

8 $2\frac{1}{2} =$ **9** $1\frac{4}{5} =$ **10** $3\frac{1}{3} =$

11 $2\frac{7}{8} =$ **12** $3\frac{4}{9} =$ **13** $5\frac{5}{6} =$

BIG IDEAS in MATH Grade 6

Change each mixed number to an improper fraction. Then divide by multiplying by the reciprocal.

14 $\frac{3}{4} \div 1\frac{1}{2} =$

15 $\frac{5}{6} \div 2\frac{1}{4} =$

16 $\frac{1}{5} \div 1\frac{3}{4} =$

17 $\frac{2}{3} \div 3\frac{1}{5} =$

18 $\frac{5}{8} \div 2\frac{3}{8} =$

19 $\frac{4}{9} \div 3\frac{3}{5} =$

20 $2\frac{1}{3} \div \frac{2}{5} =$

21 $1\frac{7}{8} \div \frac{1}{2} =$

22 $3\frac{1}{4} \div \frac{2}{3} =$

23 $2\frac{6}{7} \div \frac{1}{4} =$

24 $1\frac{5}{9} \div \frac{7}{12} =$

25 $4\frac{4}{5} \div \frac{3}{10} =$

26 $2\frac{1}{2} \div 1\frac{3}{4} =$

27 $1\frac{1}{4} \div 1\frac{5}{8} =$

28 $1\frac{2}{3} \div 2\frac{5}{6} =$

29 $5\frac{2}{3} \div 2\frac{1}{3} =$

30 $2\frac{2}{5} \div 6\frac{3}{4} =$

31 $2\frac{1}{8} \div 2\frac{5}{8} =$

Answer each question.

32 The answers to questions 14–19 above should all be fractions less than 1. The answers to questions 20–25 should all be mixed numbers greater than 1. Explain why.

_____

_____

_____

33 Explain how you could do the division in question 20 above using the distributive property. (Hint: Don't change $2\frac{1}{3}$ to an improper fraction.)

_____

_____

_____

UNIT 4

53

Dividing Fractions to Solve Problems

You can divide fractions and mixed numbers to solve many types of word problems. Division situations include measurement conversions, rate calculations, and dividing a quantity equally.

Read this problem. Answer each question.

Quinn rode his bike $4\frac{3}{4}$ miles from his house to the river. The ride took $\frac{5}{12}$ of an hour. What was his average speed in miles per hour?

Speed = Distance ÷ Time

1 Speed is a rate that you can calculate if you know the distance and the time. Which number is the dividend? _____ Which number is the divisor? _____

2 What calculation will give Quinn's average speed? _____

3 What is $4\frac{3}{4}$ written as an improper fraction? _____

4 Write the division as multiplication by the reciprocal. _____

5 Cancel common factors and multiply. Write the answer as a mixed number. _____

6 Explain how you changed the answer to a mixed number. _____

_____

7 Explain why the answer is greater than $4\frac{3}{4}$ miles per hour. _____

_____

● INDEPENDENT PRACTICE

Solve each problem. Show your work. Answer each question.

8 A pan of chocolate fudge weighed $\frac{4}{5}$ pound. It was cut into pieces that weighed $\frac{1}{10}$ pound each. How many pieces of fudge were there?

_____

9 A puppy weighs $7\frac{1}{3}$ pounds. If 1 kilogram = $2\frac{1}{5}$ pounds, what is the puppy's mass (weight) in kilograms?

_____

54   **BIG IDEAS in MATH**   Grade 6

10 A hiking trail is $2\frac{3}{4}$ miles long. If 1 kilometer $= \frac{5}{8}$ mile, what is the hiking trail's length in kilometers?

_____

11 Estella hiked $\frac{2}{3}$ of the $2\frac{3}{4}$-mile trail. Her hike took $\frac{5}{6}$ of an hour. What was Estella's average speed in miles per hour?

_____

12 Temperatures in degrees Celsius can be converted to Fahrenheit temperatures using the formula $F = \frac{9}{5}C + 32$. What is the Celsius equivalent of a temperature of $39\frac{1}{2}°F$?

_____

13 The water bottle in Sophie's class had 5 gallons of water at 9:00 A.M. By 11:45 A.M., it had $3\frac{3}{8}$ gallons left. At what rate in gallons per hour were the students drinking the water?

_____

14 Explain how you found your answer to question 13 above.

_____

_____

_____

15 A pepper plant grew from $2\frac{3}{4}$ inches to $6\frac{1}{8}$ inches in height. If 1 centimeter $= \frac{2}{5}$ inch, explain how you could find the plant's height increase in centimeters.

_____

_____

_____

Unit 4 Review

Write the reciprocal of each fraction, whole number, or mixed number.

1 $\frac{5}{7}$ **2** 16   **3** $3\frac{1}{2}$ **4** $2\frac{4}{5}$

Write the division sentence shown by each area model. Then solve.

5 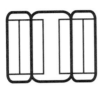   **6** 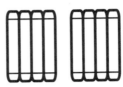   **7**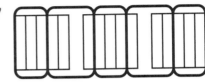

_____   _____   _____

8 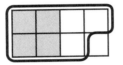   **9** 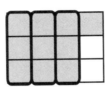   **10**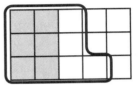

_____   _____   _____

Rewrite each division as multiplication by the reciprocal. Then solve. Write your answers as fractions or mixed numbers in lowest terms.

11 $4 \div \frac{1}{2} =$ **12** $6 \div \frac{3}{8} =$ **13** $8 \div \frac{5}{6} =$

14 $\frac{1}{4} \div \frac{2}{3} =$ **15** $\frac{5}{8} \div \frac{3}{4} =$ **16** $\frac{7}{9} \div \frac{1}{3} =$

17 $\frac{2}{3} \div 5 =$ **18** $\frac{3}{8} \div 6 =$ **19** $\frac{12}{5} \div 8 =$

20 $2\frac{1}{2} \div \frac{1}{4} =$ **21** $1\frac{5}{6} \div \frac{5}{12} =$ **22** $\frac{4}{5} \div 1\frac{3}{10} =$

BIG IDEAS in MATH Grade 6

23 $\frac{1}{3} \div 2\frac{1}{6} =$

24 $1\frac{1}{5} \div 2\frac{1}{10} =$

25 $2\frac{4}{9} \div 3\frac{2}{3} =$

26 $4\frac{1}{2} \div 1\frac{1}{3} =$

27 $3\frac{3}{5} \div 1\frac{5}{7} =$

28 $2\frac{1}{4} \div 3 =$

Solve each problem. Show your work. Answer the question.

29 Scientists were studying a 6-gram sample of rock from Mars. The sample was divided into pieces that each had a mass of $\frac{3}{5}$ gram. Into how many pieces was the rock sample divided?

_____

30 The area of a rectangle is $4\frac{2}{3}$ square inches. If the width of the rectangle is $\frac{5}{6}$ inch, what is its length?

_____

31 A truck engine held $12\frac{1}{2}$ liters of engine oil, but $7\frac{3}{8}$ liters leaked out. If 1 gallon = $3\frac{3}{4}$ liters, how many gallons of oil were left in the engine?

_____

32 Explain how you found your answer to question 31 above.

_____

_____

_____

Ratios

A **ratio** is a comparison of two numbers, for example, 5 to 4. A ratio is often written with a colon, like 5:4, or as a fraction, like $\frac{5}{4}$.

Read this problem. Answer each question.

Look at these circles and squares.

Circles to squares: _____

Squares to circles: _____

Circles to total shapes: _____

Total shapes to circles: _____

Squares to total shapes: _____

Total shapes to squares: _____

1 How many circles are there? _____   **2** How many squares are there? _____

3 What is the ratio of circles to squares? On the line above, write the ratio using *to*, a colon, and as a fraction.

4 What is the ratio of squares to circles? Write the ratio in three forms on the line above.

5 How are the ratios in questions 4 and 5 alike? How are they different? Explain.

_____

_____

6 What is the total number of shapes? _____

7 What is the ratio of circles to total shapes? Write the ratio in three forms on the line above.

8 Write the last three ratios on the answer lines above.

⬤ INDEPENDENT PRACTICE

List all six ratios for each set of squares. Write each ratio in one form only.

9   gray to white: _____   gray to total: _____   white to total: _____

white to gray: _____   total to gray: _____   total to white: _____

10   gray to white: _____   gray to total: _____   white to total: _____

white to gray: _____   total to gray: _____   total to white: _____

58   **BIG IDEAS in MATH**   Grade 6

Draw a picture using circles and triangles to show each ratio.

11 The ratio of circles to triangles is 4:3.

12 The ratio of triangles to total shapes is $\frac{5}{8}$.

13 The ratio of triangles to circles is 3 to 2.

14 The ratio of total shapes to circles is $\frac{12}{7}$.

Find each ratio. Answer each question.

15 A pond has 5 frogs and 12 tadpoles. What is the ratio of tadpoles to frogs? _____

16 There were 4 red balloons and 6 blue balloons at a party. What was the ratio of red balloons to total balloons? _____

17 In question 16, the ratio of red balloons to total balloons is not in lowest terms. Explain why this ratio is not in lowest terms. (Hint: Write the ratio as a fraction.)

_____

_____

_____

18 Mark has 4 quarters, 5 dimes, and 6 nickels. What is the ratio of total coins to quarters? _____

19 Explain how you found your answer to question 18.

_____

_____

20 If there are *c* cats and *d* dogs, what is the result of multiplying the ratio of cats to dogs by the ratio of dogs to cats? (Hint: Write the ratios as fractions.)

_____

_____

UNIT 5

59

Equivalent Ratios

You can find **equivalent ratios** the same way you find equivalent fractions. To find a ratio in **lowest terms,** write the ratio as a fraction, then divide the numerator and denominator by their greatest common factor (GCF).

Read this problem. Answer each question.

In the figure at the right, what is the ratio of shaded squares to unshaded squares in lowest terms?

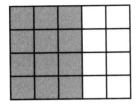

1 How many of the squares are shaded? _____

2 How many of the squares are unshaded? _____

3 What is the ratio of shaded to unshaded squares? Write the ratio as a fraction. _____

4 What is the greatest common factor (GCF) of the numerator and denominator? _____

5 Divide the numerator and denominator by the GCF: _____

6 Write the reduced ratio in three different forms: _____

7 To rewrite a ratio in **higher** terms, **multiply** the numerator and denominator by the same number. By what number would you multiply the terms of $\frac{3}{2}$ to rewrite it as $\frac{12}{8}$? Explain.

_____

_____

 INDEPENDENT PRACTICE

Write each ratio in higher terms.

8 $\frac{3}{4} \times \frac{5}{5} =$

9 $\frac{2}{5} \times \frac{6}{6} =$

10 $\frac{8}{3} \times \frac{4}{4} =$

11 $\frac{1}{2} = \frac{}{6}$

12 $\frac{5}{4} = \frac{10}{}$

13 $\frac{9}{2} = \frac{}{12}$

14 $\frac{2}{3} =$

15 $\frac{3}{8} =$

16 $\frac{7}{5} =$

BIG IDEAS in MATH   **Grade 6**

Write each ratio in lower terms.

17 $\frac{9}{12} \div \frac{3}{3} =$

18 $\frac{15}{5} \div \frac{5}{5} =$

19 $\frac{20}{12} \div \frac{2}{2} =$

20 $\frac{6}{10} = \frac{3}{}$

21 $\frac{36}{24} = \frac{}{6}$

22 $\frac{25}{30} = \frac{}{6}$

23 $\frac{18}{24} =$

24 $\frac{16}{36} =$

25 $\frac{15}{12} =$

Write each ratio in lowest terms. You may want to write each ratio as a fraction first.

26 8 to 2

27 3:9

28 7 to 14

29 16:12

30 20 to 25

31 24:20

Solve each problem. Show your work. Answer each question.

32 At recess, the ratio of students playing soccer to students not playing soccer was 12 to 20. Write this ratio in higher terms and in lowest terms.

33 There are 16 unfolded shirts in a laundry basket. There are 6 folded shirts in a stack. Write the ratio of total shirts to folded shirts in higher terms and in lowest terms.

34 Explain how you found your answer to question 33.

_____

_____

_____

35 Manesh reduced the ratio 120:72 to lowest terms. Alex reduced the ratio 72:120 to lowest terms. How are their answers related? Explain.

_____

_____

_____

UNIT 5

More Ratios

Ratios between two numbers appear in many real-life problem situations.

Read this problem. Answer each question.

A pet store sells two kinds of hamsters: golden hamsters and dwarf hamsters. The ratio of golden hamsters to dwarf hamsters, in lowest terms, is 3 to 2.

$$\frac{3}{2} = \frac{?}{10} \quad \begin{matrix} \leftarrow \\ \leftarrow \end{matrix} \quad \begin{matrix} \text{Golden hamsters} \\ \text{Dwarf hamsters} \end{matrix}$$

1 What is the ratio of dwarf hamsters to golden hamsters? _____

2 What is the ratio of golden hamsters to total hamsters? _____

3 What is the ratio of total hamsters to dwarf hamsters? _____

4 The actual number of golden hamsters in the store must be divisible by _____.

5 The actual total number of hamsters in the store must be divisible by _____.

6 Explain how you found the answer to question 5. _____

_____

_____

7 If there are 10 dwarf hamsters in the store, how many golden hamsters are there? _____

8 Explain how you found the answer to question 7. _____

_____

_____

⬤ INDEPENDENT PRACTICE

For each situation, find the named ratios in lowest terms. Show your work.

9 A string of holiday lights has 24 bulbs. Sixteen are red and the rest are green.

Red to green: Green to total: Total to red:

_____   _____   _____

10 A bowl holds 6 peaches, 7 apricots, and 8 plums.

Plums to peaches: Apricots to total: Total to peaches:

_____   _____   _____

BIG IDEAS in MATH   Grade 6

Answer each question.

11 The ratio of sharpened pencils to unsharpened pencils in a drawer is 1:3. What is the ratio of unsharpened pencils to total pencils? Explain how you found your answer.

_____

_____

_____

12 In question 11, what number is the total number of pencils divisible by? Explain how you know.

_____

_____

13 A vase contains carnations and roses. The ratio of carnations to total flowers is 3:5. What number is the number of roses divisible by? Explain how you know.

_____

_____

14 In question 13, if there are 30 flowers in all, how many roses are there? Explain how you found your answer.

_____

_____

_____

15 In one orchestra, the ratio of string instruments to woodwinds is 5 to 4, and the ratio of woodwinds to brass instruments is 3 to 2. If there are 16 brass instruments, how many woodwinds and strings are there? Explain how you found your answer.

_____

_____

_____

_____

For each given ratio, use words to describe a real-life situation the ratio could represent.

16 4:1 _____

17 3 to 4 _____

18 $\frac{2}{9}$ _____

Ratio Tables

A **ratio table** shows equivalent ratios arranged in a pattern. If you know one ratio in the table, you can find missing terms in the other ratios.

Read this problem. Answer each question.

At a pumpkin patch, visitors can buy 2 pumpkins for 5 dollars. The table shows this ratio.

Number of Pumpkins	2	4		
Price (in dollars)	5		15	40

1   What is the ratio of the number of pumpkins to the price in dollars? _____

2   What number is 2 multiplied by to get 4 pumpkins? _____

3   Multiply the price, $5, by the same number. What is the cost of 4 pumpkins? _____

4   What number is the price of $5 multiplied by to get $15? _____

5   How many pumpkins would cost $15? _____

6   How many pumpkins would cost $40? _____

7   Explain how you found the answer to question 6. _____

_____

_____

⬤ INDEPENDENT PRACTICE

Complete each ratio table by filling in the missing terms.

8

1			
4	8	20	60

9

3		12	
2	4		20

10

5	10	15	
8			80

11

		20	30
1	3		6

12

		24	
10	15	40	100

13

		28	35
3	6		15

BIG IDEAS in MATH   Grade 6

Answer each question.

14 Suppose the ratio table in question 8 is extended by one column. Give two numbers that you could use to fill in that extra column. Explain how you found the numbers.

_____

_____

15 Are any of the ratios in the table in question 13 in lowest terms? Explain.

_____

_____

Solve each problem. Answer the question.

16 Ethan is making a snack mix of raisins and almonds in a 4:3 ratio by weight. If he adds 9 ounces of almonds, how many ounces of raisins should he add? If Ethan adds 16 ounces of raisins, how many ounces of almonds should he add? Complete the table.

Ounces of Raisins			
Ounces of Almonds			

17 At a pizza shop, the ratio of cheese pizzas sold to pepperoni pizzas sold is 6 to 5. If 40 pepperoni pizzas are sold, how many cheese pizzas are sold? If 72 cheese pizzas are sold, how many pepperoni pizzas are sold? Complete the table.

Cheese Pizzas			
Pepperoni Pizzas			

18 In a certain country, the ratio of lions to tigers to bears is 5:2:3. Complete the table.

Lions	5	10		
Tigers	2		10	
Bears	3			27

19 Explain how you found the number of lions to write in the last column of the table for question 18.

_____

_____

_____

_____

Using Ratios to Solve Problems

Ratios can be used to solve many types of real-life problems.

Read this problem. Answer each question.

On a spelling quiz, Wendy spelled 17 words correctly, and 3 words incorrectly. At this rate, how many words would Wendy spell correctly on a test with 100 words?

1 What was the total number of words on the quiz? _____

2 What was the ratio of correct words to total words? _____

3 Explain why you need to find an equivalent ratio with a denominator of 100.

_____

_____

4 What number should the numerator and denominator of $\frac{17}{20}$ be multiplied by? _____

5 How many words would Wendy spell correctly on a test with 100 words? _____

6 Peter solved the problem by finding a ratio that is equivalent to $\frac{3}{20}$. Explain how Peter's method works. _____

_____

 INDEPENDENT PRACTICE

Solve each problem. Show your work. Answer each question.

7 A basketball team's win/loss ratio for the season was 2:1. If the team won 12 games, how many games did they lose?

_____

8 At a copy shop one day, the ratio of black-and-white copies to color copies printed was 9 to 2. If 1,200 color copies were printed, how many black and white copies were printed?

_____

BIG IDEAS in MATH Grade 6

9 In a bicycle race, Katy rode 12 kilometers in the time that Maci rode 9 kilometers. At this pace, how far will Maci ride in the time that Katy rides 80 kilometers?

_____

10 On a ranch, the ratio of black sheep to white sheep is 3:10. If there are a total of 390 sheep on the ranch, how many of them are black?

_____

11 A recipe for cornbread calls for $1\frac{1}{2}$ cups of cornmeal and 1 cup of flour. Krista is making a large batch of cornbread, so she used 6 cups of cornmeal. How much flour should she use?

_____

12 A bag contains red, blue, and green candies. Benjamin poured out a handful and counted 10 red, 6 blue, and 14 green candies. According to these ratios, if the bag contains a total of 400 candies, about how many of them are blue?

_____

13 Explain how you found your answer to question 10.

_____

_____

_____

14 A soup recipe calls for 6 cups of water and 4 cups of chicken broth. If you had only 3 cups of chicken broth, explain how you could find the amount of water to use.

_____

_____

_____

Unit 5 Review

List all six ratios for this set of squares. Write each ratio in one way only.

1

gray to white: _____ gray to total: _____ white to total: _____

white to gray: _____ total to gray: _____ total to white: _____

Find each ratio.

2 Chuck baked 12 cookies with nuts and 7 cookies without nuts. What was the ratio of cookies with nuts to total cookies? _____

3 Selena saw 25 ducks, 8 geese, and 4 swans on a pond. What was the ratio of ducks to total birds? _____

Write each ratio in higher terms.

4 $\frac{7}{3} \times \frac{3}{3} =$

5 $\frac{2}{3} = \frac{18}{}$

6 $\frac{6}{5} =$

Write each ratio in lower terms.

7 $\frac{16}{20} \div \frac{2}{2} =$

8 $\frac{30}{18} = \frac{}{6}$

9 $\frac{24}{40} =$

Write each ratio in lowest terms. You may want to write each ratio as a fraction first.

10 4:2

11 3 to 15

12 16:6

13 15:18

14 30 to 21

15 15 to 24

For each situation, find the named ratios in lowest terms. Show your work.

16 A box contains 40 apples and 20 oranges.

Oranges to apples: Apples to total: Total to oranges:

_____   _____   _____

17 A house has 25 windows, and 10 of them are open.

Open to closed: Closed to total: Total to open:

_____   _____   _____

BIG IDEAS in MATH Grade 6

Complete each ratio table by filling in the missing terms.

18

6	9		
2		5	12

19

		63	81
5	20		45

Solve each problem. Show your work. Answer each question.

20 At a swimming pool, Tyrone saw 6 people dive off the diving board and 8 people jump off the diving board. At this rate, if 30 people dive off the diving board, how many will jump off?

_____

21 Last season, Julia's soccer team made 9 penalty kicks and missed 6 penalty kicks. At this rate, if they attempt a total of 25 penalty kicks this season, how many will they make?

_____

22 A telemarketer made a total of 42 telephone calls. Of these calls, 12 were answered by a person, 24 were answered by an answering machine, and the rest were not answered at all. At this rate, if the telemarketer makes a total of 350 telephone calls, how many will not be answered by a person?

_____

23 Explain how you found your answer to question 22.

_____

_____

_____

24 In a 5-kilometer run/walk event, some people are running and the rest are walking. The ratio of runners to walkers is 4:3. What is the total number of people divisible by? Explain.

_____

_____

_____

Rates and Unit Rates

A **rate** is a ratio that compares quantities with different units. If the comparison is to 1 unit, it is called a **unit rate.** You can find unit rates by dividing.

Read this problem. Answer each question.

An airplane flew 28 miles in 4 minutes. What was its average speed in miles per minute?

The ratio is $\frac{28 \text{ miles}}{4 \text{ minutes}}$.

1 Explain why the ratio $\frac{28 \text{ miles}}{4 \text{ minutes}}$ is a rate. _____

_____

2 What is the greatest common factor (GCF) of 28 and 4? _____

3 Write a division sentence to divide the terms of the ratio by the GCF of the numerator and denominator. _____

4 What is $\frac{28 \text{ miles}}{4 \text{ minutes}}$ reduced to lowest terms? _____

5 Explain why this ratio in lowest terms is a unit rate. _____

_____

6 Explain how you can find the unit rate by dividing. _____

_____

7 At this rate, how far would the airplane fly in 20 minutes? Explain how you found your answer.

_____

_____

_____

● INDEPENDENT PRACTICE

Tell whether each ratio is a rate or not.

8 $\frac{5 \text{ gallons}}{120 \text{ miles}}$ _____

9 $\frac{16 \text{ hours}}{9 \text{ hours}}$ _____

10 $\frac{3 \text{ inches}}{12 \text{ inches}}$ _____

11 $\frac{40 \text{ meters}}{6 \text{ seconds}}$ _____

BIG IDEAS in MATH Grade 6

Find the unit rate for each situation.

12 Henry caught 12 fish in 4 hours. _____

13 A baby elephant gained 150 pounds in 60 days. _____

14 Marisa paid $3.00 for 6 pounds of oranges. _____

15 It took Jack 30 seconds to climb a 20-foot cliff. _____

Solve each problem. Show your work. Answer the question.

16 A 12-ounce jar of jelly costs $2.40. A 16-ounce jar of jelly costs $4.00. Which jar of jelly costs less per ounce?

_____

17 A duck flew 210 miles in 6 hours. A goose flew 250 miles in 8 hours. Which bird flew at the fastest average speed?

_____

18 Between 1:30 P.M. and 1:50 P.M., 40 gallons of water leaked into a boat. At what rate in gallons per hour was the water leaking into the boat?

_____

19 Dirk drove his car 75 miles on 3 gallons of gas. Trina drove her car 76 miles on 4 gallons of gas. Cassandra drove her car 125 miles on 5 gallons of gas. Whose cars got the same mileage in miles per gallon?

_____

20 In question 19, what was Dirk's mileage in miles per gallon? What was his mileage in gallons per mile? Explain how the rate in miles per gallon is related to the rate in gallons per mile.

_____

_____

_____

UNIT 6

Equivalent Rates and Rate Tables

Two rates are **equivalent** if they simplify to the same unit rate. You can arrange several equivalent rates in a **rate table.**

Read this problem. Answer each question.

Elliot made a batch of pancake batter. It was enough to make 16 large pancakes. He used 2 cups of flour in the recipe.

Number of Pancakes		16	32	
Cups of Flour	1	2		7

1 What is the ratio of number of pancakes to cups of flour? _____

2 Explain why this ratio is a rate. _____

3 What is the unit rate? _____

4 How did you find the unit rate? _____

_____

5 Fill in the blank spaces in the rate table above.

6 Explain how you found the missing numbers in the table.

_____

_____

● INDEPENDENT PRACTICE

Complete each rate table. Describe the rule you use to complete it.

7

Kilometers	60		240	
Hours	1	2		10

Rule: _____

_____

8

Dollars	1	5	10	
Apples		20		100

Rule: _____

_____

9

Liters	4		24	36
Seconds		12		27

Rule: _____

_____

BIG IDEAS in MATH Grade 6

Use the rate described to complete each rate table.

10 Cheryl bought 1 pound of cheese for $6.00.

Pounds				
Dollars				

11 Oscar skateboarded 3 miles in 45 minutes.

Miles				
Minutes				

Find the unit rate in each problem. Then solve. Show your work. Answer the question.

12 A sailboat traveled 16 kilometers in 2 hours. At this rate, how far could it travel in 5 hours?

_____

13 If 4 apples cost $1.00, what would be the cost of 10 apples?

_____

14 A recipe that makes 5 cups of soup calls for 2 teaspoons of salt. How much salt would be needed for 20 cups of soup?

_____

15 If 5 liters of paint covers an area of 40 square meters, how much paint is needed to cover an area of 100 square meters?

_____

16 Hiro walked slowly for 30 minutes, then more quickly for 60 more minutes. If he walked 2 kilometers in the first 30 minutes, what can you conclude about the total distance he walked? Explain your reasoning.

_____

_____

_____

Representing Rates

A rate describes a relationship that can be shown in a graph by a straight line.

Read this problem. Answer each question.

The graph shows how the cost of organic broccoli depends on the amount purchased.

What is the broccoli's price per pound?

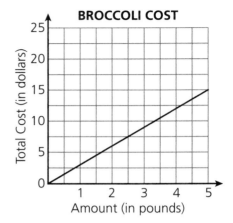

1 The line contains the point (5, 15). What does this tell you about the cost of broccoli?

_____

_____

2 The point (5, 15) describes a rate. Write this rate as a fraction. _____

3 What is the price per pound of the broccoli? _____

4 Explain how you found the price per pound. _____

_____

5 How much would it cost for 2.2 pounds of broccoli? _____

6 Explain why the line on the graph is a straight line. _____

_____

● INDEPENDENT PRACTICE

Find the unit rate for the situation shown in each graph.

7
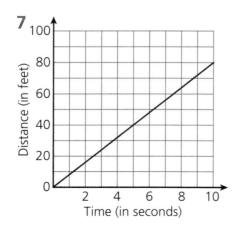

8
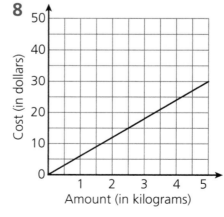

9
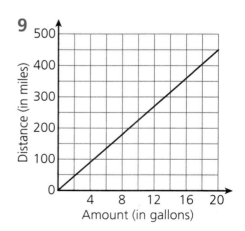

_____   _____   _____

BIG IDEAS in MATH Grade 6

Follow the directions. Answer each question.

10 Draw a line on the graph to represent the rate in this rate table.

Volume (in cubic inches)	20	40	60	80	100
Weight (in pounds)	4	8	12	16	20

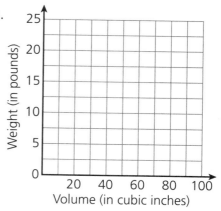

11 Amy's class went on a camping trip. The teacher drove in her car at 60 miles per hour, and the students rode in a school bus at 50 miles per hour. They left at the same time.

Complete this rate table to compare the progress of the car and the bus. Then graph each rate on the same coordinate grid. Label the lines "Car" and "Bus."

Time (in hours)	0.5	1	1.5	2	2.5
Car Distance (in miles)					
Bus Distance (in miles)					

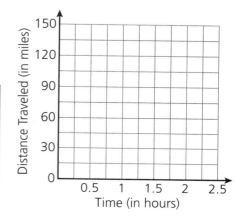

12 How far ahead of the bus was the car after 2 hours? Explain how you found your answer.

_____

_____

_____

13 The total distance to the lake was 180 miles. How much longer did the bus take than the car to get to the lake? Explain how you found your answer.

_____

_____

_____

Using Rates to Solve Problems

Many real-life problems can be solved using rates. Finding the unit rate is often the first step.

Read this problem. Answer each question.

Use your centimeter ruler to help you solve this problem.

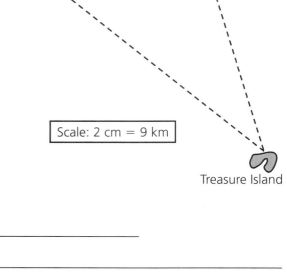

Gull Island

Black Island

Treasure Island

Scale: 2 cm = 9 km

The scale map shows three small islands in a lake. How much farther from Gull Island is Treasure Island than Black Island?

1 What is the rate in this problem?

_____

2 What distance does 1 centimeter represent on the map?

_____

3 How far is it from Gull Island to Black Island? _____

4 Explain how you found the answer to question 3. _____

_____

5 How far is it from Gull Island to Treasure Island? _____

6 How much farther from Gull Island is Treasure Island than Black Island? _____

7 A boat took 3 hours to go from Treasure Island to Black Island. Explain how you could find the boat's average speed.

_____

_____

● INDEPENDENT PRACTICE

Solve each problem. Show your work. Answer the question.

8 Marco is riding his bicycle at a speed of 16 kilometers per hour. How far will he ride in 2 hours at this speed?

_____

BIG IDEAS in MATH Grade 6

9 Serena read 15 pages of a book in 20 minutes. At this rate, how many pages will she read in 60 minutes?

_____

10 At a gift shop, Luke saw a sign reading "5 seashells for $1.00." What would be the cost of 12 seashells?

_____

11 When Ed turned the oven on at 4:30 P.M., the oven temperature was 75°F. By 4:35 P.M., the temperature had risen to 225°F. At this rate, what will the oven temperature be at 4:41 P.M.?

_____

12 Ms. Blanco drove her car at a speed of 80 kilometers per hour for $1\frac{1}{2}$ hours, then at a speed of 100 kilometers per hour for $2\frac{1}{2}$ hours. How far did she drive in all?

_____

13 In question 12 above, what was Ms. Blanco's average speed for the entire drive?

_____

14 Kyle is using two garden hoses to fill a wading pool with water. One hose is supplying 5 gallons of water per minute, and the other hose is supplying 3 gallons per minute. How long will it take to fill the pool with 100 gallons of water?

_____

15 In question 13 above, Ms. Blanco's average speed is **not** equal to 90 kilometers per hour (the average of 80 kilometers per hour and 100 kilometers per hour). Explain why.

_____

_____

_____

UNIT 6

77

Unit 6 Review

Tell whether each ratio is a rate or not.

1 $\dfrac{35 \text{ dollars}}{6 \text{ kilograms}}$ _____

2 $\dfrac{15 \text{ seconds}}{45 \text{ seconds}}$ _____

Find the unit rate for each situation.

3 A mouse's tail grew 9 millimeters in 3 months. _____

4 The airplane flew 300 miles in $\frac{1}{2}$ hour. _____

Use the rate described to complete each rate table.

5 I bought 8 pounds of beans for $4.

Pounds				
Dollars				

6 The car used 4 gallons of gas to go 100 miles.

Gallons				
Miles				

Follow the directions.

7 Draw a line on the graph to represent the rate in this rate table.

Amount of Paint (in gallons)	1	2	3	4	5
Area (in square feet)	400	800	1,200	1,600	2,000

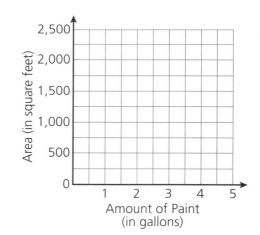

Solve each problem. Show your work. Answer the question.

8 Rafael skated 100 yards in 20 seconds. Roger skated 150 yards in 25 seconds. Who skated at a faster rate of speed?

_____

BIG IDEAS in MATH   Grade 6

9 In question 8, Roger skated 150 yards in 25 seconds. How far could he skate in 1 minute at this rate?

_____

10 A 400-milliliter bottle of soy sauce costs $3.00. A 600-milliliter bottle of soy sauce costs $4.00. Which bottle costs less per milliliter?

_____

11 If 6 pounds of ham cost $48, how much ham would cost $20?

_____

12 Explain how you found your answer to question 11.

_____

_____

_____

13 Use your centimeter ruler to help you solve this problem. Amalia bicycled from Brockton to Maples, then to Stenson, then back to Brockton. How far did she ride in all?

Brockton Stenson
Maples
Scale: 5 centimeters = 20 kilometers

_____

14 In question 13, if the ride took Amalia a total of 3 hours, what was her average speed?

_____

15 In question 13, Amalia rode at the same speed all the way from Brockton to Stenson. How was her riding time from Brockton to Maples related to her riding time from Maples to Stenson? Explain.

_____

_____

_____

UNIT 6 **79**

Variables and Expressions

An **algebraic expression** can contain numbers, variables, and operations.

Read this problem. Answer each question.

The length of this rectangle is hidden. The algebraic expression 3*l* represents the area of the rectangle.

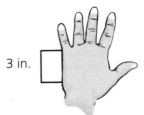

3 in.

1 How do you find the area of a rectangle?

_____

2 A **constant** is a known or unchanging number in an expression. What is the constant in this expression? _____

3 What does the constant represent in the expression? _____

4 A **variable** is a letter or other symbol that stands for an unknown or changing number. What is the variable in the expression? _____

5 What does the variable represent in the expression? _____

6 When you multiply a variable by a number, the multiplication sign is usually left out. Write the expression above using a multiplication sign. _____

7 What do you need to know to find the area of the rectangle?

_____

 INDEPENDENT PRACTICE

Identify each quantity as a constant (a known value that does not change) or a variable (an unknown value, or a value that changes).

8 the number of hours in a day _____

9 the number of hours Joe sleeps each night _____

10 the number of ounces in a pound _____

11 the number of ounces of food a cat eats in a day _____

12 the cost in dollars of a gallon of milk _____

BIG IDEAS in MATH Grade 6

Write each algebraic expression in words. Use the phrase *a number* for each variable.

13 $x + 4$ _____

14 $s - 7$ _____

15 $5n$ _____

16 $\dfrac{t}{6}$ _____

17 $9 + c$ _____

18 $10 - a$ _____

19 $\dfrac{1}{5}x$ _____

20 $\dfrac{2}{w}$ _____

Describe a real-life situation that each expression could represent.

21 $y + 6$ _____

_____

22 $x - 20$ _____

_____

23 $4g$ _____

_____

24 $\dfrac{\$100}{n}$ _____

_____

Answer the question.

25 In question 21, what is the variable in the expression? What is the constant? What do the variable and constant stand for in the situation you described?

_____

_____

_____

Writing Expressions

Many expressions in words can be written as algebraic expressions. Certain words give clues about the operation to use.

Read this problem. Answer each question.

There are c chocolate cookies. The number of peanut cookies is 5 more than the number of chocolate cookies. The number of oatmeal cookies is 3 less than the number of chocolate cookies. The number of vanilla cookies is double the number of chocolate cookies. The chocolate cookies will be shared equally by 8 people.

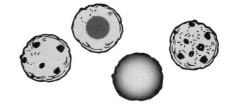

1 What does the variable c stand for? _____

2 What operation is used to show "five more than"? _____

3 What operation is used to show "three less than"? _____

4 What does "double the number" mean? _____

5 What operation is used to show the number being shared equally? _____

6 Write an algebraic expression for each situation in terms of chocolate cookies.

Peanut cookies: _____   Oatmeal cookies: _____

Vanilla cookies: _____   Cookies shared: _____

7 Identify each expression in question 6 as a sum, difference, product, or quotient. Write the name on the line after the expression.

INDEPENDENT PRACTICE

Choose a variable and write an algebraic expression for each verbal expression.

8 a number divided by 5 _____   **9** a number increased by 14 _____

10 nine times a number _____   **11** twelve less than a number _____

12 two more than a number _____   **13** a number decreased by 3.5 _____

14 twice a number _____   **15** a number split into 4 equal parts _____

16 half of a number _____   **17** five fewer than a number _____

18 triple a number _____   **19** one-fourth of a number _____

Write an algebraic expression to represent the answer to each question.

20 What is 6 plus x? _____

21 What is 5 times y? _____

22 What is z divided by 7? _____

23 What is n minus 11? _____

24 What is the sum of s and 10? _____

25 What is the difference of t and 9? _____

26 What is the product of 8 and x? _____

27 What is the quotient of w and 5? _____

28 There are 12 eggs in a dozen. How many eggs are in d dozen? _____

29 Eva is y years old. Gwen is 5 years older than Eva. What is Gwen's age in years? _____

30 Sanjay hiked the same distance each day for 4 days. He hiked m miles in all. How many miles did Sanjay hike each day? _____

31 Olivia is 8 centimeters shorter than Diana. If Diana is d centimeters tall, what is Olivia's height in centimeters? _____

32 Cheese costs $6 per pound. What is the cost in dollars of p pounds of cheese? _____

33 The temperature was 45°F at dawn. By noon, it was k degrees warmer. What was the temperature in degrees Fahrenheit at noon? _____

Answer each question.

34 The expression "eight more than n" can be written as $n + 8$. Can it also be written as $8 + n$? Explain.

_____

_____

35 The expression "four less than n" can be written as $n - 4$. Can it also be written as $4 - n$? Explain.

_____

_____

36 The expression "one-third of x" can be written as $\frac{1}{3}x$. Can it also be written as $\frac{x}{3}$? Explain.

_____

_____

Evaluating Expressions

To **evaluate** an algebraic expression, replace the variable in the expression by the given number. Then carry out the operation.

Read this problem. Answer each question.

The price of a ticket is $6. The cost of n tickets can be found with the expression $6n$.

n	$6n$
1	
2	
3	
10	

1 What is the variable in the expression? _____

2 Complete: If $n = 1$, then $6n =$ _____ × _____ = _____.

3 Complete: If $n = 2$, then $6n =$ _____ × _____ = _____.

4 If $n = 3$, what is the value of $6n$? _____

5 If $n = 10$, what is the value of $6n$? _____

6 Fill in the table to show the value of this expression for the different values of n.

7 Jeremy and Rachel are going to substitute different values for n into the expression $6n$. Is it possible that they will get the same result? Explain.

_____

_____

⬤ INDEPENDENT PRACTICE

Evaluate each expression for $x = 8$. Show your work.

8 $x + 3$

9 $x - 7$

10 $2x$

11 $\frac{x}{2}$

12 $10 + x$

13 $15 - x$

14 $5x$

15 $\frac{24}{x}$

16 $x + 1.5$

17 $x - 8$

18 $\frac{1}{4}x$

19 $\frac{8}{x}$

BIG IDEAS in MATH   Grade 6

Evaluate each expression for the given value of the variable.

20 $n = 10$ **a** $2 + n$ **b** $n - 2$ **c** $2n$ **d** $\frac{n}{2}$

21 $k = 3$ **a** $k + 12$ **b** $12 - k$ **c** $12k$ **d** $\frac{12}{k}$

22 $p = 4$ **a** $p + 16$ **b** $16 - p$ **c** $16p$ **d** $\frac{16}{p}$

Complete each table by evaluating the given expression for each value of the variable.

23

x	$3x$
1	
2	
3	
4	

24

x	$x + 5$
0	
1	
2	
3	

25

x	$x - 6$
10	
12	
14	
16	

26

x	$\frac{x}{5}$
5	
10	
15	
20	

27

x	$10 - x$
1	
2	
5	
10	

28

x	$\frac{1}{3}x$
0	
1	
2	
3	

29

x	$\frac{15}{x}$
1	
3	
5	
15	

30

x	$x + 0.5$
2	
4	
6	
8	

Answer the question.

31 Look at the tables you completed in questions 25 and 27 above. In question 25, as x gets larger, $x - 6$ gets larger. In question 27, as x gets larger, $10 - x$ gets smaller. Explain why this difference exists.

_____

_____

_____

UNIT 7

Equivalent Expressions

Equivalent expressions represent the same value in different forms. Use the **commutative, associative,** and **distributive properties** to rewrite expressions in equivalent forms.

Read this problem. Answer each question.

This model shows three different rectangles with lengths of x units, 5 units, and $x + 5$ units and a width of 4 units.

1 What is the area of a rectangle with length x and width 4? _____

2 What is the area of a rectangle with length 5 and width 4? _____

3 What is the area of a rectangle with length $(x + 5)$ and width 4? _____

4 According to the distributive property, $4(x + 5) = 4x + 20$.
   How do your answers to questions 1–3 confirm this? Explain. _____

   _____

   _____

5 Use the commutative property $(a + b = b + a)$ to rewrite $4x + 20$. _____

6 What is the perimeter of a rectangle
   with length $(x + 5)$ and width 4? _____

7 Use the associative property $((a + b) + c = a + (b + c))$ to rewrite $(x + 5) + 4$. _____

8 If $x = 7$, what are the area and perimeter of the total rectangle? Explain.

   _____

   _____

● INDEPENDENT PRACTICE

Use the commutative property to rewrite each expression.

9 $a + 5$ **10** $y + 7$ **11** $4 + x$ **12** $8 + z$

13 $t \times 6$ **14** $w \times \frac{2}{5}$ **15** $9 \times s$ **16** $0.7 \times p$

Use the associative property to rewrite each expression.

17 $(b + 2) + 6$

18 $(10 + x) + 5$

19 $7 + (y + 4)$

20 $4 \times (7 \times a)$

21 $(k \times 16) \times 25$

22 $100 \times (m \times 0.65)$

Use the distributive property to rewrite each expression.

23 $3(x + 5)$

24 $8(a + 1)$

25 $2(5 + t)$

26 $4(y - 6)$

27 $6(2 - n)$

28 $10(r + \frac{1}{2})$

29 $\frac{1}{3}(z + 12)$

30 $0.5(c - 8)$

31 $x(4 + 6)$

Write three or more equivalent expressions for each of the described quantities.

32 The area of this rectangle:

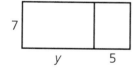

_____

_____

33 The area of this rectangle:

_____

_____

34 The perimeter of this square:

_____

_____

Answer the question.

35 Look at this equation: $(n - 5) - 2 = n - (5 - 2)$. Choose a value for n and see if the equation is true. What does the result tell you about the associative property for subtraction? Explain.

_____

_____

_____

UNIT 7

87

Simplifying Expressions

To **simplify an algebraic expression** means to write it in simplest form.
For example, $2x + 3x + 7 + 2$ can be simplified to $5x + 9$.

Read this problem. Answer each question.

The picture shows a regular pentagon. The length
of one side is given as an expression.

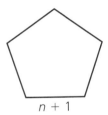

$n + 1$

1 What does it mean to say this pentagon is *regular?* _____

2 Add the side lengths to get an
expression for the perimeter. _____

3 Simplify $n + n + n + n + n$. _____ **4** What is $1 + 1 + 1 + 1 + 1$? _____

5 Combine your answers to questions 3 and 4 to
get the simplified expression for the perimeter. _____

6 The pentagon has 5 equal sides, each with length $(n + 1)$.
Use multiplication to write another expression for the perimeter. _____

7 How does the distributive property relate the answers to questions 5 and 6? Explain.

_____

_____

⬤ INDEPENDENT PRACTICE

Each figure below is a regular polygon. For each one, write an expression for the perimeter by
adding the sides. Then write an equivalent expression using multiplication.

8 $x + 1$ _____ _____

9 $2y$ _____ _____

10 $z + 3$ _____ _____

BIG IDEAS in MATH Grade 6

Simplify each expression.

11 $5n + 2n$

12 $6y + 3y + 2$

13 $7x - 3x$

14 $x + 4 + x + 3$

15 $4y + y + 7 - 1$

16 $10z + 3 - 4z + 2$

17 $5 + 7a + 3 - a$

18 $3x - 4 + 3x + 4$

19 $6m - 2m + 5m$

Write an addition expression for the perimeter of each rectangle. Then simplify each expression.

20 5 ▭
$x + 2$
_____

21 4 ▭
$y - 1$
_____

22 3 ▭
$5z$
_____

Answer each question.

23 Explain why the expression $5n + 2n$ can be written as $n(5 + 2)$. Then explain why the expression $n(5 + 2)$ is the same as $7n$.

_____

_____

_____

24 The perimeter of a rectangle with length l and width w is given by the formula $P = 2l + 2w$. Use this method to write an expression for the perimeter of the rectangle in question 20. Then simplify the expression to show that it is equivalent to the one you found in question 20.

_____

_____

_____

UNIT 7

89

Using Expressions to Solve Problems

Many real-life problems can be solved using algebraic expressions.

Read this problem. Answer each question.

Rob bought 3 packs of trading cards, and Ted bought 4 packs of trading cards. If n is the number of cards in each pack, what expression names the total number of cards Rob and Ted bought?

1 Write an expression for the number of trading cards that Rob bought. _____

2 Write an expression for the number of trading cards that Ted bought. _____

3 Add and simplify to get an expression for the total number of trading cards. _____

4 If $n = 6$, use your expression to find the total number of trading cards. _____

5 Explain how you found the total number of trading cards. _____

_____

6 If $n = 6$, how many trading cards did Rob buy? How many did Ted buy? Explain how these answers are related to your answer to question 4.

_____

_____

INDEPENDENT PRACTICE

Follow the directions and answer each question.

7 Demi grew 5 centimeters last summer. At the beginning of summer, her height was h centimeters.

   a Write an expression for her height at the end of summer. _____

   b If $h = 142$, how tall was Demi at the end of summer? _____

8 Each side of an equilateral triangle measures $5s$ inches.

   a Write an addition expression for the perimeter of the triangle. _____

   b Simplify the expression. _____

   c If $s = 4$, what is the perimeter of the triangle? _____

BIG IDEAS in MATH Grade 6

9 A square has a perimeter of 36 feet. Each side of the square measures $3n$ feet.

   a What is the value of n? _____

   b Explain how you found the value of n. _____

   _____

10 At a yard sale, books cost x dollars each. Keisha bought 7 books and Max bought 5 books.

   a Write an addition expression for the total cost of their books. _____

   b Simplify the expression. _____

   c If $x = 0.75$, what was the total cost of the books they bought? _____

   d Explain how you found the total cost of the books. _____

   _____

   _____

11 At the yard sale, CDs cost y dollars each. Max bought 7 CDs and Keisha bought 3 CDs.

   a Write an expression to show how much **_more_** Max spent on CDs than Keisha. _____

   b Simplify the expression. _____

   c If $y = 1.5$, how much more did Max spend on CDs than Keisha? _____

12 A rectangle has length $(k + 5)$ centimeters and width $(k - 2)$ centimeters.

   a Write an expression for the perimeter of the rectangle.

   _____

   b Simplify the expression. _____

   c If $k = 6$, what is the perimeter of the rectangle? _____

   d Would it be possible for k to equal 2 in this problem? Explain why or why not.

   _____

   _____

Unit 7 Review

Identify each quantity as a constant or a variable.

1 the number of days in a week _____

2 the number of days in a family vacation _____

Write each algebraic expression in words. Use the phrase *a number* for each variable.

3 $n + 8$ _____   **4** $k - 3$ _____

5 $4x$ _____   **6** $\frac{w}{9}$ _____

Choose a variable and write an algebraic expression for each verbal expression.

7 two more than a number _____   **8** one less than a number _____

9 one-eighth of a number _____   **10** a number divided by four _____

Write an algebraic expression to represent the answer to each question.

11 Jack is j years old. His younger brother Peter is 8 years old. What is the difference in years between their ages? _____

12 There are 16 ounces in 1 pound. How many ounces are there in k pounds? _____

13 Three friends shared n candies equally. How many candies did each get? _____

14 Zia has n nickels, d dimes, and 6 quarters. How many coins does she have? _____

Complete each table by evaluating the given expression for each value of the variable.

15

x	$x + 7$
0	
3	
7	
20	

16

x	$x - 4$
4	
5	
8	
10	

17

x	$8x$
0	
1	
2	
3	

18

x	$\frac{6}{x}$
1	
2	
6	
12	

BIG IDEAS in MATH Grade 6

Simplify each expression.

19 $8y + y$

20 $5z + 3 + 2z + 1$

21 $9a - 3a + 8$

22 $7x + 5 - x + 2$

23 $2n + 3n - 2n$

24 $5k + 7 - 5k - 4$

Write three or more equivalent expressions for each of the described quantities.

25 The area of this rectangle:

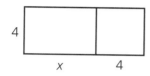

_____

_____

26 The perimeter of this equilateral triangle:

2x + 3

_____

_____

Follow the directions and answer each question.

27 Viktor built 4 birdhouses. Shakeel built 6 birdhouses. Each birdhouse required n nails.

a Write and simplify an expression for the total number of nails they used. _____

b If $n = 14$, how many nails did they use in all? _____

c Suppose 1 extra nail was used to hang up each birdhouse. How would this change the expression for the total number of nails used?

_____

_____

28 Delia earned d dollars last summer. Pilar earned 20 dollars more than Delia. Jade earned 5 dollars less than Delia.

a Write and simplify an addition expression for the total number of dollars the three friends earned last summer. _____

b If $d = 60$, what was the total amount the three friends earned? _____

c If Pilar earned n dollars last summer, write an expression for the number of dollars Jade earned. Explain how you found your answer.

_____

_____

Equations

An **equation** is a number sentence that says two algebraic expressions are equal. (One of the expressions is often just a number.) Many real-life situations can be represented by equations.

Read this problem. Answer each question.

Loreen bought some T-shirts on sale for 5 dollars each. The equation below describes this situation.

$$5n = 30$$

1 What are the two expressions in this equation? _____

2 What word can the = sign be translated into? _____

3 Explain why $5n = 30$ is an equation. _____

_____

4 If one T-shirt costs 5 dollars, what does the expression $5n$ represent? _____

_____

5 The equation $5n = 30$ can be translated simply as "five times a number is 30." How can it be translated in terms of this situation involving Loreen buying T-shirts?

_____

_____

6 How many T-shirts did Loreen buy? Explain how you know your answer is correct.

_____

_____

INDEPENDENT PRACTICE

Translate each equation into a statement in words.

7 $8n = 40$ _____

8 $x + 6 = 15$ _____

9 $\frac{y}{3} = 25$ _____

10 $m - 14 = 60$ _____

11 $9x = 120$ _____

12 $d - 5 = 7.5$ _____

13 $z + \frac{1}{4} = \frac{3}{4}$ _____

14 $\frac{10}{a} = 2$ _____

15 $\frac{1}{3}y = 11$ _____

16 $0.4t = 0.6$ _____

Describe a real-life situation that each equation could represent.

17 $4n = 12$ _____

_____

18 $w + 5 = 20$ _____

_____

19 $\frac{c}{4} = 6$ _____

_____

20 $a - 8 = 10$ _____

_____

Answer each question.

21 Explain the difference between an expression and an equation.

_____

_____

_____

22 Look at the equation $n + 3 = 10$. Is this equation true when $n = 5$? Is it true when $n = 7$? Explain how you found your answers.

_____

_____

_____

Writing Equations

Many real-life problem situations can be represented by equations. The unknown value is represented by a variable like *n* or *x.* Words like *more than, less than, twice, half, double, sum, difference, product,* and *quotient* tell you which operation is involved.

Read this problem. Answer each question.

Half of a certain number is 16. What equation represents this relationship?

1 Choose a variable to represent the unknown number. _____

2 What operation and value would you use to find half of a number? _____

3 What expression represents half of the unknown number? _____

4 Write an equation to show that half of the unknown number is 16. _____

5 What is the unknown number? Explain how you found your answer. _____

_____

6 Jake is twice as old as Sam, who is 16 years old. Can this situation be represented by the equation you wrote in question 4? What would the variable stand for? Explain.

_____

_____

_____

● INDEPENDENT PRACTICE

Write an equation to represent each relationship described below.

7 Four more than a number *n* equals 13. _____

8 Six less than a number *k* equals 28. _____

9 Three times a number *x* equals 15. _____

10 A number *n* divided by 5 is equal to 10. _____

11 The sum of *s* and 7 is 33. _____

12 The difference between *t* and 16 is 5. _____

13 The product of 0.75 and *y* is 4.5. _____

BIG IDEAS in MATH   Grade 6

14 The quotient of z and 4 is 6. _____

15 Twice a number n equals 30. _____

16 Half of a number r is equal to 12. _____

17 Four-fifths of a number k is 2.4. _____

Write an equation to represent each real-life problem situation.

18 Brandon had s stamps in his collection. He bought 12 more, and then he had 148 in all. _____

19 There are n dozen doughnuts on a tray, for a total of 96 doughnuts. _____

20 Maya had q quarters in her purse. She spent 8 of them, and had 11 quarters left. _____

21 An apple pie weighed 32 ounces. It was cut into p pieces that weighed 4 ounces each. _____

22 Tickets to the circus cost c dollars last year. This year the price has doubled to $14. _____

23 A rope was 80 feet long. Ellis cut x feet off the rope, and now it is 64 feet long. _____

Answer each question.

24 Explain how you found your equation in question 18 above.

_____

_____

25 Explain how you found your equation in question 19 above.

_____

_____

26 In question 19, is there only one value of n that makes your equation true? Explain.

_____

_____

Solving Equations: Addition and Subtraction

To **solve an equation** means to find the value of the variable that makes the equation true. You can solve some equations by **adding** the same number to both sides of the equation to get the variable by itself. You can solve other equations by **subtracting** the same number from both sides of the equation.

Read this problem. Answer each question.

The balance scale shows the equation $x + 3 = 7$. Use the balance scale to solve the equation for x.

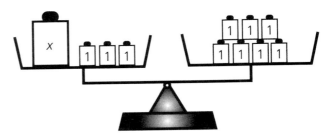

1   What expression is represented by the blocks on the left side of the balance? _____

2   What expression is represented by the blocks on the right side of the balance? _____

3   Why is the balance scale shown in balance? _____

4   If you remove 3 of the 1s from the left side of the balance, what will remain? _____

5   If you remove 3 of the 1s from the right side of the balance, what will remain? _____

6   What value of x makes the equation true? _____   In other words, $x =$ _____.

7   What mathematical operation is the same as removing 3 of the 1s from each side of the scale?

_____

8   Check your solution from question 6 above by substituting your value for x into the equation. Does this value for x make the equation true? Explain.

_____

_____

● INDEPENDENT PRACTICE

Write the equation represented by each balance scale. Then solve the equation.

9

_____

_____

BIG IDEAS in MATH   Grade 6

10

_____

_____

11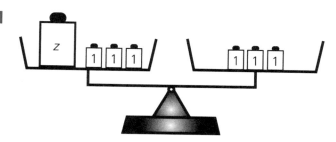

_____

_____

Identify the operation that must be performed on both sides of each equation to solve it.

12 $a + 6 = 14$ _____

13 $b - 4 = 22$ _____

14 $8 + c = 13$ _____

15 $d - 12 = 7$ _____

Solve each equation by adding or subtracting the same number on both sides. Show your work.

16 $x + 2 = 8$

17 $m + 7 = 7$

18 $y - 3 = 9$

19 $6 + z = 13$

20 $p - 6 = 11$

21 $w + 15 = 40$

22 $a - 0.5 = 3.5$

23 $k + \frac{1}{4} = \frac{3}{4}$

24 $j - \frac{1}{6} = 2\frac{5}{6}$

Answer each question.

25 What type of equation can be solved by adding the same number to both sides? Explain.

_____

_____

26 What type of equation can be solved by subtracting the same number from both sides? Explain.

_____

_____

Solving Equations: Multiplication and Division

Some equations can be solved by **multiplying** or **dividing** both sides of the equation by the same number. If the variable is multiplied by a certain number, divide both sides by that number. If the variable is divided by a certain number, multiply both sides by that number.

Read this problem. Answer each question.

The balance scale shows the equation $3x = 6$.
Use the balance scale to solve the equation for x.

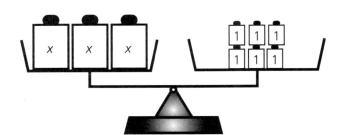

1   What expression is represented by the blocks on the left side of the balance? _____

2   What expression is represented by the blocks on the right side of the balance? _____

3   If you divide the three x blocks into 3 equal groups, what is in each group? _____

4   If you divide the six 1 blocks into 3 equal groups, what is in each group? _____

5   What is the solution to the equation? _____

6   Explain how to solve the equation $3x = 6$ by dividing both sides by a certain number.

_____

_____

7   Check your solution from question 5 above by substituting your value for x into the equation. Does this value for x make the equation true? Explain.

_____

_____

⬤ INDEPENDENT PRACTICE

Write the equation represented by each balance scale. Then solve the equation.

8

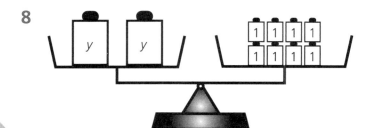

_____

_____

9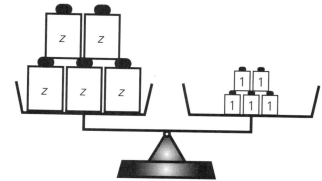

_____

_____

Identify the operation that must be performed on both sides of each equation to solve it.

10 $7a = 35$ _____

11 $\frac{b}{4} = 8$ _____

12 $0.3c = 9.6$ _____

13 $\frac{d}{15} = 2$ _____

Solve each equation by multiplying or dividing both sides by the same number. Show your work.

14 $6x = 18$

15 $\frac{y}{2} = 10$

16 $10z = 50$

17 $\frac{n}{6} = 4$

18 $2w = 7$

19 $\frac{t}{3} = 1$

20 $5s = 3$

21 $\frac{k}{0.5} = 8$

22 $9x = 0$

Answer each question.

23 Explain how you found your answer to question 15 above.

_____

_____

24 Charlie solved the equation $4x = 24$ by dividing both sides by 4. Melissa solved the same equation by multiplying both sides by $\frac{1}{4}$. Are both methods correct? Explain.

_____

_____

UNIT 8

Solving Equations with Fractions

To solve an equation in which the variable is multiplied by a fraction, multiply both sides of the equation by the **reciprocal** of the fraction.

Read this problem. Answer each question.

Astrid paid $12 for $\frac{3}{5}$ pound of shrimp. The equation at the right can be solved to find y, the price per pound.

$$\frac{3}{5}y = 12$$

1 What is the result of multiplying a fraction by its reciprocal? _____

2 What is the reciprocal of $\frac{3}{5}$? _____

3 Multiply both sides of the equation by the reciprocal of $\frac{3}{5}$. What is the result? _____

4 Check your solution from question 3 by substituting your value for y into the equation. Does this value for y make the equation true? Explain.

_____

5 You can also solve this equation by dividing both sides by $\frac{3}{5}$. How does this method relate to the method you used above? Explain.

_____

_____

⬤ **INDEPENDENT PRACTICE**

Translate each equation into a statement with words.

6 $\frac{1}{4}n = 5$ _____

_____

7 $\frac{2}{3}x = 6$ _____

_____

8 $\frac{1}{6}w = \frac{3}{4}$ _____

_____

9 $\frac{7}{3}y = 8$ _____

_____

BIG IDEAS in MATH Grade 6

Each of these equations can be solved by multiplying both sides by the reciprocal of the fraction. For each equation, identify the reciprocal to multiply by.

10 $\frac{3}{4}a = 7$

11 $\frac{5}{12}k = 9$

12 $\frac{1}{5}x = 3$

13 $\frac{7}{4}y = 3$

14 $\frac{1}{2}p = \frac{4}{5}$

15 $\frac{11}{2}q = \frac{11}{4}$

Solve each equation by multiplying both sides by the reciprocal of the fraction. Show your work.

16 $\frac{2}{3}x = 6$

17 $\frac{4}{5}y = 8$

18 $\frac{1}{3}z = 4$

19 $\frac{4}{3}a = 20$

20 $\frac{9}{2}b = 9$

21 $\frac{1}{8}c = \frac{1}{2}$

22 $\frac{2}{5}r = 1$

23 $\frac{7}{3}s = 0$

24 $\frac{3}{2}t = \frac{3}{4}$

Answer each question.

25 Explain how you found your answer to question 18 above.

_____

_____

26 Explain how you found your answer to question 24 above.

_____

_____

27 The equation $0.75x = 7$ can be solved by multiplying both sides by a certain fraction. Explain.

_____

_____

UNIT 8

103

Using Equations to Solve Problems

Many types of word problems can be solved by writing and solving an equation.

Read this problem. Answer each question.

Lulu bought a box of *n* beads for making jewelry. She used 24 of the beads to make a necklace, and there were 136 left in the box. How many beads were in the box to start with?

1 What does the variable *n* represent? _____

2 What operation represents Lulu using 24 beads? _____

3 Write an equation that can be solved for *n*. _____

4 Solve your equation. Show your work. _____

5 How many beads were in the box to start with? _____

6 Explain how you solved your equation in question 4 above. _____

_____

⬤ INDEPENDENT PRACTICE

Write and solve an equation for each problem. Show your work.

7 Mr. Armstrong bought *p* packages of hot dogs. Each package contained 8 hot dogs. If Mr. Armstrong bought a total of 72 hot dogs, how many packages did he buy?

_____

8 Patricia wrote 7 thank-you cards on Saturday and *t* more thank-you cards on Sunday. She wrote 20 thank-you cards in all. How many thank-you cards did Patricia write on Sunday?

_____

9 There are *n* sixth-grade students at Parkview School, and they are divided into 4 equal classes. Each class has 27 students. How many sixth-graders are there in all?

_____

10 Twenty-five less than a number m is 63. What is the value of m?

_____

11 Chad used to earn d dollars per hour. Last week, his pay rate was increased by $2.50 per hour, and now he earns $14.25 per hour. What was Chad's pay rate before last week?

_____

12 Anna's hair was h inches long. After she cut $1\frac{1}{2}$ inches off, it was $8\frac{1}{4}$ inches long. How long was Anna's hair before she cut it?

_____

13 A bag of kitten food has a net weight of 2.4 pounds. Tara bought k bags, for a total of 14.4 pounds of kitten food. How many bags did she buy?

_____

14 Five friends bought a cake for c dollars and shared the cost equally. Each friend paid $3.50. What was the total cost of the cake?

_____

Describe a real-life problem that could be solved using each equation.

15 $x + 6 = 15$ _____

16 $12n = 108$ _____

Answer the question.

17 Compare this problem to the problem in question 10 above: "Twenty-five more than a number n is 63. What is the value of n?" Explain why the value of n is 50 less than the value of m in question 10.

_____

_____

_____

Unit 8 Review

Translate each equation into a statement in words.

1 $n - 11 = 18$ _____

2 $\frac{z}{5} = 2.6$ _____

Write an equation to represent each relationship described below.

3 Five more than a number n is 14. _____

4 Twice a number j is equal to 36. _____

5 One-third of a number x is $2\frac{1}{2}$. _____

Write an equation to represent each real-life problem situation.

6 A building had n windows, but 15 of them broke in an earthquake. There were 76 windows unbroken. _____

7 A shark swam at 5.3 meters per second for t seconds. It swam 100 meters in all. _____

8 A cake weighed w ounces. It was cut into 12 pieces, and each piece weighed $1\frac{3}{4}$ ounces. _____

Solve each equation by using the same operation on both sides. Show your work.

9 $k - 7 = 10$ **10** $m + 2 = 8$ **11** $r - 1.5 = 3$

12 $t + \frac{2}{3} = 3\frac{2}{3}$ **13** $4x = 32$ **14** $\frac{y}{5} = 3$

15 $3z = 16$ **16** $\frac{s}{12} = \frac{1}{4}$ **17** $\frac{5}{6}m = 10$

18 $\frac{3}{4}n = 15$ **19** $\frac{1}{5}p = 6$ **20** $\frac{8}{3}z = \frac{1}{2}$

BIG IDEAS in MATH Grade 6

Write and solve an equation for each problem. Show your work.

21 There were n nuts on a tree. A squirrel ate 40 of them, and 85 nuts remained. How many nuts were on the tree to start with?

_____

22 A building was h feet tall. A new roof added 15 feet to the height, making the building 120 feet tall. How tall was the building before the new roof was added?

_____

23 Eric built k ship models in 6 years. He built 4 ship models each year. How many ship models did Eric build in all?

_____

24 Inez fed the neighbor's dog $\frac{2}{3}$ pound of food per day for t days while the neighbors were on vacation. The dog ate a total of 8 pounds of food. How many days were the neighbors on vacation?

_____

Answer each question.

25 Explain how you found your answer to question 24 above.

_____

_____

_____

26 The equation $2x + 5 = 19$ can be solved in two steps, beginning with a subtraction. Explain how you could solve this equation.

_____

_____

_____

Formulas

A **formula** is an algebraic equation that expresses an important mathematical relationship. You can **evaluate** a formula by substituting known values for the variables and then simplifying.

Read this problem. Answer each question.

What is the circumference of this circle?

16 cm

Circumference = pi × diameter
$C = 3.14 \times d$

1 What do C and d stand for in the formula $C = 3.14 \times d$? _____

2 The number 3.14 is an approximation of pi, sometimes written π. The number pi is a constant. What is a constant?

_____

3 What is the diameter of the circle? _____

4 What value should be substituted for d in the formula? _____

5 What is the circumference of the circle? _____

6 Explain how you found the circumference. _____

_____

 ## INDEPENDENT PRACTICE

Substitute the given values into the formula to find the perimeter or circumference of each figure.

7 10 in. [square]

$P = 4s$

$P = 4 \times$ _____

$P =$ _____

8   5 ft

$C = 3.14 \times d$

$C = 3.14 \times$ _____

$C =$ _____

9 6 cm [rectangle] 9 cm

$P = 2l + 2w$

$P = 2 \times$ _____ $+ 2 \times$ _____

$P =$ _____

Find the perimeter of each figure described below. Show your work.

10 a square with side 5 meters

11 a rectangle with length 7 feet and width $4\frac{1}{2}$ feet

Find the circumference of each circle described below. Show your work.

12 a circle with diameter 12 centimeters

13 a circle with diameter 1.5 inches

Use the formula $d = r \times t$ to find the distance traveled in each example below. Show your work.

14 rate = 20 miles per hour; time = 4 hours

15 rate = 60 meters per sec.; time = 2.5 sec.

Write and solve the formula needed for each problem. Show your work. Answer the question.

16 A tablecloth is shaped like a rectangle measuring 8 feet by 6 feet. What is the perimeter of the tablecloth?

_____

17 A circular window measures 80 centimeters in diameter. What is the circumference of the window?

_____

18 Jenny had some square tiles measuring 12 inches on each side. She put four of the tiles together to make a larger square. What was the perimeter of the larger square?

_____

19 Logan walked at a speed of 75 meters per minute for 4 minutes. Then he rode his scooter at a speed of 250 meters per minute for 3 minutes. How far did Logan travel in all?

_____

20 The diameter of a circle is always twice the radius. If you know the radius of a circle, explain how you can find the circumference.

_____

_____

UNIT 9

109

Area Formulas

The **area** of a geometric figure is the number of square units inside it. You can calculate the area of many figures using formulas.

Read this problem. Answer each question.

What is the area of this triangle?

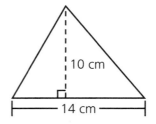

Area = $\frac{1}{2}$ base × height

$A = \frac{1}{2}bh$

10 cm

14 cm

1 What do *b* and *h* stand for in this formula? _____

2 What is the base of the triangle? _____

3 What is the height of the triangle? _____

4 Use the formula to find the area of the triangle. _____

5 What would be the area of a rectangle measuring 14 centimeters by 10 centimeters? How would its area be related to the area of the triangle above? Explain.

_____

_____

● INDEPENDENT PRACTICE

Substitute the given values into the formula to find the area of each figure.

6   9 ft

$A = s \times s$

$A = $ _____ × _____

$A = $ _____

7   7 m

16 m

$A = lw$

$A = $ _____ × _____

$A = $ _____

8
8 in.

11 in.

$A = \frac{1}{2}bh$

$A = \frac{1}{2} \times$ _____ × _____

$A = $ _____

Find the area of each figure described below. Show your work.

9 a square with side 12 inches

10 a rectangle with length 15 meters and width 10 meters

BIG IDEAS in MATH Grade 6

Find the area of each triangle described below. Show your work.

11 a triangle with base 6 feet and height 7 feet

12 a triangle with base 5 meters and height 3 meters

Write and solve the formula needed for each problem. Show your work. Answer the question.

13 Each side of a square painting is 20 inches long. What is the area of the painting?

_____

14 A rectangular soccer field measures 110 meters by 60 meters. What is the area of the soccer field?

_____

15 The base of a triangle is 8 centimeters. The height of the triangle is twice the base. What is the area of the triangle?

_____

16 This figure is composed of three squares measuring 6 inches by 6 inches. What is the total area of the figure?

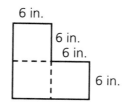

6 in.

6 in.
6 in.

6 in.

_____

17 Rectangle *PQRS* measures 9 centimeters by 16 centimeters. What is the area of triangle *PRS*?

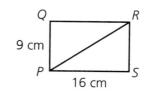

Q *R*

9 cm

P *S*

16 cm

_____

18 Explain how you found your answer to question 17.

_____

_____

_____

UNIT 9

Volume Formulas

The **volume** of a geometric figure is the number of cubic units inside it. You can calculate the volume of many figures using formulas.

Read this problem. Answer each question.

What is the volume of this rectangular prism?

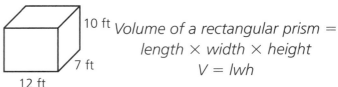

Volume of a rectangular prism =
length × width × height
$$V = lwh$$

1 What is the length of the rectangular prism? _____

2 What is the width of the rectangular prism? _____

3 What is the height of the rectangular prism? _____

4 Use the formula to find the volume of the rectangular prism. Show your work.

_____

5 When you find the volume of a rectangular prism, does it matter in which order you multiply the length, width, and height? Explain.

_____

● INDEPENDENT PRACTICE

Substitute the given values into the formula to find the volume of each figure.

6

$V = s \times s \times s$

$V =$ ___ $\times$ ___ $\times$ ___

$V =$ _____

7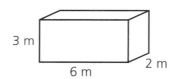

$V = lwh$

$V =$ ___ $\times$ ___ $\times$ ___

$V =$ _____

8

$V = lwh$

$V =$ ___ $\times$ ___ $\times$ ___

$V =$ _____

Find the volume of each figure described below. Show your work.

9 a cube with side 10 inches

10 a rectangular prism with length 9 feet, width 2 feet, and height 6 feet

11 a cube with side 2.5 centimeters

12 a rectangular prism with length $\frac{1}{2}$ mile, width $\frac{1}{4}$ mile, and height 1 mile

Write and solve the formula needed for each problem. Show your work. Answer the question.

13 A suitcase shaped like a rectangular prism is 30 inches long, 20 inches wide, and 10 inches tall. What is its volume?

_____

14 Connor has a puzzle that is a cube measuring 7 centimeters on each side. What is the volume of this cube?

_____

15 A fish tank is shaped like a rectangular prism measuring 2 meters by 1.5 meters by 1.4 meters. The tank is $\frac{1}{2}$ full of water. What is the volume of the water in the fish tank?

_____

16 The base of a rectangular prism is a square measuring 8 inches on each side. The height of the prism is 7.5 inches. What is the volume of the prism?

_____

17 A pizza box measures $1\frac{1}{2}$ feet by $1\frac{1}{2}$ feet by 4 inches. What is its volume in cubic inches?

_____

18 How many 3-centimeter cubes can fit into this box?

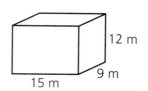

12 m
9 m
15 m

_____

19 Explain how you found your answer to question 18.

_____

_____

Using Formulas to Solve Problems

Some problems require you to solve a formula for an unknown quantity. Substitute the given values into the formula. Then solve the way you would solve any equation.

Read this problem. Answer each question.

The perimeter of a rectangle is 42 inches. If the rectangle's width is 8 inches, what is its length?

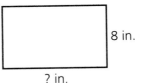

8 in.

? in.

1 What is the formula for the perimeter of a rectangle? _____

2 Which variable in the formula is 42 inches?
Which variable in the formula is 8 inches? _____

3 Substitute 42 and 8 into the formula. What is the resulting equation? _____

4 To solve this equation for *l*, start by subtracting
16 from both sides. What is the result? _____

5 Now divide both sides by 2. What is the solution? _____

6 If you knew the area of a rectangle and its width, how would you find the length? Explain.

_____

_____

⬤ **INDEPENDENT PRACTICE**

Find the missing dimension (length or width) of each rectangle. Show your work.

7 area = 60 square feet; length =
10 feet; width = ?

8 perimeter = 24 centimeters; width =
5 centimeters; length = ?

Find the missing rate or time in these distance-rate-time situations. Show your work.

9 distance = 75 miles; time = 3 hours;
rate = ?

10 distance = 60 meters; rate = 12 meters
per second; time = ?

BIG IDEAS in MATH Grade 6

Find the missing dimension (length, width, or height) of each rectangular prism. Show your work.

11 volume = 30 cubic centimeters; length = 5 centimeters; width = 2 centimeters; height = ?

12 volume = 180 cubic feet; length = 15 feet; height = 3 feet; width = ?

Write and solve the formula to solve each problem. Show your work. Answer the question.

13 A rectangular postcard has an area of 96 square centimeters. If the postcard is 12 centimeters long, how wide is it?

_____

14 A cereal box is 8 inches long and 3 inches wide. If the box has a volume of 240 cubic inches, how tall is it?

_____

15 Natalie went down a hill on her sled. She traveled 120 yards in 15 seconds. What was her average speed in yards per second?

_____

16 Mr. Burney's front lawn is shaped like a square with a perimeter of 44 meters. What is the area of the lawn?

_____

17 A rectangular computer screen has a perimeter of 60 inches. If the length of the screen is 18 inches, what is its area?

_____

18 Explain how you found your answer to question 17.

_____

_____

_____

UNIT 9

Unit 9 Review

Substitute the given values into the formula to find the perimeter, circumference, area, or volume of each figure.

1
3 in.
7 in.

$P = 2l + 2w$

$P = 2 \times$ _____ $+ 2 \times$ _____

$P =$ _____

2
9 m

$C = 3.14 \times d$

$C = 3.14 \times$ _____

$C =$ _____

3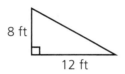
15 cm

$A = s \times s$

$A =$ _____ $\times$ _____

$A =$ _____

4
8 ft
12 ft

$A = \frac{1}{2}bh$

$A = \frac{1}{2} \times$ _____ $\times$ _____

$A =$ _____

5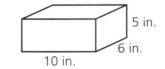
4 cm

$V = s \times s \times s$

$V =$ ___ $\times$ ___ $\times$ ___

$V =$ _____

6
5 in.
6 in.
10 in.

$V = lwh$

$V =$ ___ $\times$ ___ $\times$ ___

$V =$ _____

Solve the appropriate formula to find each missing quantity. Show your work.

7 a square with side 18 kilometers; perimeter = ?

8 rate = 35 miles per second; time = 6 seconds; distance = ?

9 a rectangle with length 6 miles and width $\frac{1}{2}$ mile; area = ?

10 a rectangular prism with length 9 feet, width 5 feet, and height 4 feet; volume = ?

11 a square with perimeter 80 centimeters; side = ?

12 a rectangle with perimeter 28 feet and length 9 feet; width = ?

13 a triangle with area 12 square inches and base 6 inches; height = ?

14 distance = 45 kilometers; rate = 9 kilometers per hour; time = ?

Write and solve the formula needed for each problem. Show your work. Answer the question.

15 A rectangular playground measures 75 yards by 35 yards. What is the perimeter of the playground?

_____

16 A train traveled at 80 kilometers per hour for 2 hours, then at 110 kilometers per hour for $\frac{1}{2}$ hour. How far did it travel in all?

_____

17 This figure is composed of a square and a triangle. What is the total area of the figure?

5 cm | 8 cm

_____

18 The perimeter of a square goldfish pond is 12 meters. What is the area of the goldfish pond?

_____

19 A bicycle tire has a circumference of 62.8 inches. What is its diameter?

_____

20 Brianna swam for 60 seconds at a speed of 3 feet per second to reach an island in a lake. Kayla swam the same distance in 90 seconds. What was Kayla's average speed?

_____

21 Explain how you found your answer to question 20.

_____

_____

_____

UNIT 9   **117**

Patterns

A **pattern** is a sequence of numbers, letters, geometric figures, or other objects that repeats or changes in a predictable way.

Read this problem. Answer each question.

Troy is making this growing pattern with the first letter in his name.

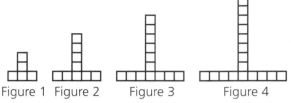

Figure 1   Figure 2   Figure 3   Figure 4

1 How many squares are in figure 1? _____ Figure 2? _____ Figure 3? _____ Figure 4? _____

2 Describe where the additional squares were placed to change each figure to the next figure.

_____

3 If you know the number of squares in one figure, how can you find the number of squares in the next figure? In other words, what is the rule for this pattern? _____

4 How many squares will there be in figure 5? _____

5 Troy says the number of squares in figure 10 will be 4 × 10 + 1, which equals 41. Explain why Troy's formula is correct.

_____

_____

● INDEPENDENT PRACTICE

Look at the geometric pattern and answer each question.

6

Figure 1   Figure 2   Figure 3   Figure 4

a How many dots will there be in figure 5? _____

b What is the rule for this pattern? _____

c How many dots will there be in figure 12? _____

d Explain how you found the number of dots in figure 12. _____

_____

BIG IDEAS in MATH Grade 6

Look at each number pattern and answer the questions.

7 5, 10, 15, 20, 25, ____, …

a What is the rule for this pattern? _____

b What will be the 6th number in the pattern? _____

c What will be the 20th number in the pattern? _____

8 2, 8, ____, 20, 26, 32, …

a What is the rule for this pattern? _____

b What will be the 3rd number in the pattern? _____

c What will be the 10th number in the pattern? _____

9 2, 6, 18, 54, 162, ____, …

a What is the rule for this pattern? _____

b What will be the 6th number in the pattern? _____

Find the next five numbers in each pattern described below.

10 First number: 3   Rule: Add 3   3, ____, ____, ____, ____, ____, …

11 First number: 4   Rule: Multiply by 2   4, ____, ____, ____, ____, ____, …

12 First number: 50   Rule: Subtract 8   50, ____, ____, ____, ____, ____, …

13 First number: 800   Rule: Divide by 2   800, ____, ____, ____, ____, ____, …

Answer each question.

14 Suppose the number pattern in question 10 describes the number of squares in a geometric pattern. In the space below, draw the first three figures in this geometric pattern.

15 How could you use multiplication to find the number of squares in figure 100 of the pattern you just drew? Explain how you know your answer is correct.

_____

_____

_____

UNIT 10

Sequences and Rules

The rule for a number pattern (or **number sequence**) or a growing geometric pattern can often be described by an algebraic expression.

Read this problem. Answer each question.

Write an algebraic expression for the number of triangles in figure *n* of this growing pattern.

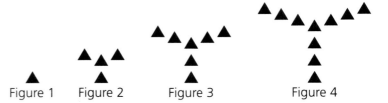

Figure 1   Figure 2   Figure 3   Figure 4

1   How many triangles are added to each figure to make the next figure? _____

2   How many triangles will there be in figure 5? _____

3   Write a number sequence that matches the number of triangles per figure. _____

4   How is this number sequence related to the number sequence 3, 6, 9, 12, 15, …?

_____

5   In a rule for a sequence, the variable *n* names the position of the number in the sequence. Write an algebraic expression for the *n*th number in the sequence 3, 6, 9, 12, 15, … . _____

6   Write an expression for the number of triangles in figure *n* of the pattern above. Use the expression you wrote in question 5 as the starting point. _____

7   Explain how you found your expression in question 6. _____

_____

⬤ INDEPENDENT PRACTICE

Look at the geometric pattern and answer the questions.

8

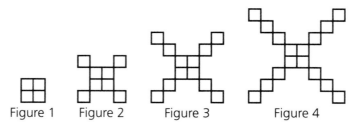

Figure 1   Figure 2   Figure 3   Figure 4

   a   What is the matching number sequence? _____

   b   How many squares will there be in figure 5? _____

c Write an algebraic expression for the number of squares in figure *n*. _____

d Explain how you found your expression for the number of squares. _____

_____

_____

Look at each number pattern and answer the questions.

9 6, 12, 18, 24, 30, ____, ... **a** What will be the 6th number in the pattern? _____

b Write an expression for the *n*th number. _____

10 ____, 30, 45, 60, 75, 90, ... **a** What was the 1st number in the pattern? _____

b Write an expression for the *n*th number. _____

11 6, 11, 16, 21, 26, ____, ... **a** What will be the 6th number in the pattern? _____

b Write an expression for the *n*th number. _____

12 1, 5, 9, 13, 17, ____, ... **a** What will be the 6th number in the pattern? _____

b Write an expression for the *n*th number. _____

c Explain how you found your expression for the *n*th number.

_____

_____

Answer each question.

13 The first row of seats in a theater has 12 seats. The number of seats in the *n*th row is given by the expression $3n + 9$.

a Write a number sequence to show
the number of seats in the first 5 rows. _____

b How many seats are in the 15th row? _____

c Can the number of seats in the *n*th row also be given by the expression $3(n + 3)$? Explain.

_____

_____

_____

_____

Function Tables

A **function table,** or input-output table, shows a relationship between two variables. The relationship can often be expressed by an algebraic equation.

Read this problem. Answer each question.

Write equations to describe the relationships shown in these two function tables.

Table 1

x	y
0	0
1	4
2	8
3	12

Table 2

x	y
0	3
1	7
2	11
3	15

1 When $x = 0$, what is the value of y in table 1? _____ In table 2? _____

2 When $x = 4$, what will be the value of y in table 1? _____ In table 2? _____

3 For any x-value in table 1, you can find the corresponding y-value by multiplying. Explain.

_____

4 Write an equation to describe the relationship between x and y in table 1. _____

5 How are the y-values in table 2 related to the y-values in table 1? _____

_____

6 Write an equation to describe the relationship between x and y in table 2. _____

7 Explain how you found your equation in question 6. _____

_____

 ## INDEPENDENT PRACTICE

Write an equation to describe the relationship shown in each function table.

8

x	y
0	0
1	5
2	10
3	15

9

x	y
0	6
2	8
7	13
10	16

10

x	y
0	5
1	8
2	11
3	14

_____ _____ _____

BIG IDEAS in MATH Grade 6

Write an equation to describe the relationship shown in each function table. Then complete each table by writing in the missing value.

11

x	y
10	7
12	9
15	12
20	17
24	

_____

12

x	y
0	1
1	7
2	13
3	
4	25

_____

13

x	y
1	8
2	18
3	28
4	38
	78

_____

Answer each question.

14 The table shows how the distance traveled by a ship is changing over time.

Time (in hours)	Distance (in miles)
0	0
1	18
2	36
3	54

  a At this rate, how far will the ship travel in 4 hours? _____

  b Write an equation to describe the relationship between t, time in hours, and d, distance in miles.

  _____

  c How long will it take the ship to travel 216 miles? Explain how you found your answer.

  _____

  _____

15 The table shows how Beth's and Kira's heights have changed over time, where x = Beth's height in centimeters and y = Kira's height in centimeters.

x	y
120	112
125	117
130	122
133	125

  a According to the table, when Beth was 128 centimeters tall, how tall was Kira? _____

  b Write an equation to describe the relationship between x and y. _____

  c What will be the value of x when $y = 140$? Explain how you found your answer.

  _____

  _____

Constructing Function Tables

You can use an equation that relates two variables to construct a function table.

Read this problem. Answer each question.

It costs $5 to rent a paddleboat, plus $3 per hour. Write an equation to show the relationship between x, the number of hours the boat is rented, and y, the total cost in dollars. Then use your equation to complete the function table.

x	y
1	
2	
3	
4	

1 What number should be multiplied by x in the equation? Explain how you know.

_____

2 Write an equation that relates x and y. _____

3 Use your equation to find the values of y when x = 1, x = 2, x = 3, and x = 4. Show your work, and write the y-values in the table above.

x = 1: _____   x = 2: _____

x = 3: _____   x = 4: _____

4 How much would it cost to rent a paddleboat for 8 hours? _____

5 Explain how you found your answer to question 4. _____

_____

INDEPENDENT PRACTICE

Use the equation to complete each function table.

6 $y = x + 8$

x	y
0	
2	
4	
6	

7 $y = 7x$

x	y
0	
1	
2	
3	

8 $y = 2x + 1$

x	y
0	
1	
2	
3	

9 $y = 4x - 5$

x	y
2	
4	
6	
8	

10 $y = 0.5x$

x	y
0	
4	
8	
12	

11 $y = 20 - x$

x	y
5	
10	
15	
20	

BIG IDEAS in MATH Grade 6

Answer each question.

12 Every skateboard at Beppo's Board Shop is on sale for $10 off the regular price.

   a Write an equation that describes the relationship between
x, the regular price in dollars, and y, the sale price in dollars. _____

   b Use your equation to complete this function table.

x	y
40	
49	
59	
75	

   c Nathan bought a skateboard on sale for $35. What was its regular price? Explain how you found your answer.

_____
_____
_____

13 Ms. Pacitti is buying chalk for her classroom. Each box contains 8 pieces of chalk.

   a Write an equation to show the relationship between x, the
number of boxes of chalk, and y, the total number of pieces of chalk. _____

   b Use your equation to complete this function table.

x	y
1	
2	
3	
4	

   c If Ms. Pacitti bought a total of 56 pieces of chalk, how many boxes of chalk did she buy? Explain how you found your answer.

_____
_____
_____

14 A taxi ride costs $1.50 plus $0.65 per mile.

   a Write an equation to relate x, the length in
miles of a taxi ride, and y, the cost in dollars. _____

   b Use your equation to complete this function table.

x	y
1	
2	
5	
10	

   c Use your equation to find the length in miles of a taxi ride that costs $6.70. Show your work.

   d A taxi driver uses a shortcut on the drive from the airport to downtown. The shortcut makes the drive 2 miles shorter. How much money does this shortcut save? How do you know?

_____
_____

UNIT 10

Look at the geometric pattern and answer each question.

1

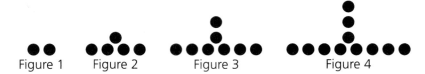

Figure 1   Figure 2   Figure 3   Figure 4

a Write the matching number pattern. _____

b How many circles will there be in figure 5? _____

c Write an algebraic expression for the number of circles in figure n. _____

d Explain how you found your algebraic expression. _____

_____

Look at each number pattern and answer the questions.

2 5, 10, 20, 40, 80, ____, …   **a** What will be the 6th number in the pattern? _____

b What is the rule for this pattern? _____

3 8, 16, 24, ____, 40, 48, …   **a** What will be the 4th number in the pattern? _____

b What will be the 100th number in the pattern? _____

c Write an expression for the nth number. _____

4 30, 27, 24, 21, 18, ____, …   **a** What will be the 6th number in the pattern? _____

b Which number in the pattern will be 0? Explain how you found your answer.

_____

Write an equation to describe the relationship shown in each function table. Then complete each table by writing in the missing value.

5

x	y
2	1
6	3
20	
36	18

6

x	y
0	3
1	5
2	7
	23

7

x	y
1	3
2	7
3	11
20	

_____   _____   _____

BIG IDEAS in MATH Grade 6

In each problem below, use the equation to complete the function table.

8 $y = 6x$

x	y
0	
1	
2	
3	

9 $y = 4x + 2$

x	y
0	
1	
2	
3	

10 $y = 5x - 3$

x	y
2	
4	
6	
8	

Answer each question.

11 The Singh family is on vacation. The table shows how their distance from home is changing over time on the third day of their vacation.

Time (in hours)	Distance (kilometers)
0	400
1	480
2	560
3	640

a How far from home will the Singhs be after 4 hours?

_____

b Write an equation that relates x, time in hours, and y, distance in kilometers.

_____

c After how many hours will the Singh family be 1,000 kilometers from home? Show your work.

_____

12 Isaac has $60 in a savings account at a bank. He is going to earn $25 per week this summer and put all the money in the savings account.

a Write an equation to show the relationship between x, the number of weeks Isaac works, and y, the total number of dollars in his savings account.

_____

b Use your equation to complete this function table.

x	y
1	
2	
3	
4	

c Isaac wants to have a total of $335 in his savings account at the end of the summer. Use your equation to find out how many weeks he needs to work. Show your work.

_____

MATHEMATICS REFERENCE SHEET

Perimeter Formulas

Square $\qquad$ $P = 4s$

Rectangle $\qquad$ $P = 2l + 2w$ or $P = 2b + 2h$

Triangle $\qquad$ $P = a + b + c$

Area Formulas

Square $\qquad$ $A = s \cdot s$ or $A = s^2$

Rectangle $\qquad$ $A = lw$ or $A = bh$

Parallelogram $\qquad$ $A = bh$

Triangle $\qquad$ $A = \frac{1}{2}bh$

Volume Formulas

Cube $\qquad$ $V = s \cdot s \cdot s$ or $V = s^3$

Rectangular Prism $\qquad$ $V = lwh$

Surface Area Formula

Rectangular Prism $\qquad$ $SA = 2lw + 2lh + 2wh$

Circle Formulas

Circumference $\qquad$ $C = 2\pi r$ or $C = \pi d$

Area $\qquad$ $A = 2\pi r^2$

Other Formulas

Distance-rate-time $\qquad$ $D = rt$

Interest $\qquad$ $I = prt$

Conversions

3 feet = 1 yard $\qquad$ 60 seconds = 1 minute

5,280 feet = 1 mile $\qquad$ 60 minutes = 1 hour

BIG IDEAS in MATH Grade 6